D0509012

Updated Edition

Madeline Hunter's

MASTERY
TEACHING

T2-BVV-923

The Madeline Hunter Collection

Madeline Hunter. (1967). *Motivation Theory for Teachers*

Madeline Hunter. (1967). *Retention Theory for Teachers*

Madeline Hunter. (1967). *Teach More—Faster!*

Madeline Hunter. (1971). *Teach for Transfer*

Madeline Hunter. (1976). *Improved Instruction*

Madeline Hunter and Sally Breit. (1976). *Aide-ing in Education*

Madeline Hunter and Paul V. Carlson. (1977). *Improving Your Child's Behavior*

Gerda Lawrence and Madeline Hunter. (1978). *Parent-Teacher Conferencing*

Madeline Hunter. (1982). *Mastery Teaching: Increasing Instructional Effectiveness in Elementary and Secondary Schools, Colleges, and Universities*

Madeline Hunter and Doug Russell. (1989). *Mastering Coaching and Supervision*

Madeline Hunter. (1990). *Discipline That Develops Self-Discipline*

For information about the Mastery Teaching Videotapes, please contact the UCLA Instructional Media Library, Powell Library—Room 46, Los Angeles, CA 90095–1517, phone 310-206-1248.

Updated Edition

Madeline Hunter's
MASTERY TEACHING

Increasing Instructional Effectiveness
in Elementary and
Secondary Schools

Revised and Updated by
Robin Hunter

CORWIN PRESS
A Sage Publications Company
Thousand Oaks, California

© 2004 by Robin Hunter
Original edition © Copyright 1982 by Madeline Hunter.

All rights reserved. When forms and sample documents are included, their use is authorized only by educators, local school sites, and/or noncommercial entities who have purchased the book. Except for that usage, no part of this book may be reproduced or utilized in any form or by any means, electronic or mechanical, including photocopying, recording, or by any information storage and retrieval system, without permission in writing from the publisher.

For information:

Corwin Press
A Sage Publications Company
2455 Teller Road
Thousand Oaks, California 91320
www.corwinpress.com

Sage Publications Ltd.
1 Oliver's Yard
55 City Road
London EC1Y 1SP
United Kingdom

Sage Publications India Pvt. Ltd.
B-42, Panchsheel Enclave
Post Box 4109
New Delhi 110 017 India

Printed in the United States of America

Library of Congress Cataloging-in-Publication Data

Hunter, Robin, 1948-
    Madeline Hunter's Mastery teaching: Increasing instructional effectiveness in elementary and secondary schools. — Updated ed. / revised and updated by Robin Hunter.
        p. cm.
Includes bibliographical references and index.
ISBN 0-7619-3929-6 (cloth)
ISBN 0-7619-3930-X (pbk.)
    1. High school teaching. 2. Elementary school teaching. 3. Learning, Psychology of. 4. Classroom management. I. Title: Mastery teaching. II. Hunter, Madeline C. Mastery teaching. III. Title: Madeline Hunter's Mastery teaching. IV. Title.
LB1607.H854 2004
371.102—dc22

                                2004004625

This book is printed on acid-free paper.

04   05   06   07   10   9   8   7   6   5   4   3   2

Acquisitions Editor:	Faye Zucker
Editorial Assistant:	Stacy Wagner
Production Editor:	Denise Santoyo
Copy Editor:	Cheryl Duksta
Typesetter:	C&M Digitals (P) Ltd.
Indexer:	Pamela Van Huss
Cover Designer:	Tracy E. Miller
Graphic Designer:	Lisa Miller

Contents

Preface to the Updated Edition

In writing this updated version of *Mastery Teaching*, foremost in my mind was one of Hippocrates' tenets: "First, do no harm." Madeline's work in bringing the science of teaching to the art of delivery was breakthrough 40 years ago and yet is still being validated by continuing research. Her work serves as a sound platform for teacher decision making upon which current practitioners continue to build.

As did many others, I had the tremendous privilege of working closely with Madeline for many years and watched the continual refinement of translating research into practical classroom practice. First as a teacher, then as a staff developer, and currently as a principal I have seen the power of her work in increasing student achievement. I have also seen the transformation of talented individual teachers into consummate professionals who routinely use research findings to guide their practice. This has been a wonderful journey.

This revision of *Mastery Teaching* would not have been possible without the talent, knowledge and help of Doug Russell, one of Madeline's "educational children." Doug spent many hours reading, editing, and helping articulate the concepts presented here. Thank you, Doug, for not only this but for the many years I have had the opportunity to learn from you.

I would also like to thank Pat Wolfe for her valuable input into this work. In attempting to pull this all together I was fortunate to be able to use the exquisite skills of Pam Healy, whose proficiency with a computer enabled my chicken scratching to appear as a polished manuscript. Finally, I would like to thank Stacy Wagner, who provided a great deal of support to me in this project. Her superb editorial skills and time are thoroughly embedded in the book you now hold.

Madeline Hunter's work has often been misunderstood and/or misapplied. I hope that in this revision I have done no harm to an outstanding body of knowledge.

—Robin Hunter, 2004

Corwin Press thanks Patricia Wolfe and David A. Sousa for their guidance in the development of this updated edition and Cheri A. Hunter for her dedication and tireless encouragement throughout the process.

Preface to the Original Edition

This book and its accompanying series of mastery teaching videotapes were developed to increase the teaching effectiveness of those who work with teenagers and young adults. Of course, as students mature we expect them to assume increasing responsibility for their own learning. As teachers mature, it is equally their responsibility to increase those professional skills that research has demonstrated will accelerate the learning of all students. This book and set of videotapes present some teaching techniques that are applicable to all disciplines, all learners, all methodologies, and all teaching styles and personalities.

Appreciation is expressed to Dr. Andrea Rich and Dr. Vera Martinez of the UCLA Office of Instructional Development for their financial and administrative support; to Bill Wolf, Hamid Natily, and Peter Prager of the Instructional Media Center for their technical and artistic expertise; and to Margaret Devers and Lillian Ostroff, whose secretarial assistance made manuscripts and videoscripts become realities.

This book is gratefully and fondly dedicated to Margaret Devers, the superb administrative assistant who supported and assisted me for twenty years as I grew in knowledge about teaching and learning.

The ultimate reality of this venture will be your accelerating teaching effectiveness with resultant increases in successful and satisfying learning accomplishment by your students.

—Madeline Hunter, 1982

Introduction to the Original Edition

In this book and the accompanying set of mastery teaching videotapes, you will find described many teaching techniques you are already using. I learned these techniques from watching effective teachers teach. I have labeled these techniques and explained the psychological theory behind why they work. As a result, from now on you will know what you are doing when you teach, why you are doing what you do, and do that consciously and deliberately to increase your students' learning. In no way have we included all the techniques that make teachers more effective. However, as you read and view, you will find that you may add some new techniques to your repertoire of effective teaching skills.

The book and tapes of mastery teaching were designed to be used for either group discussion or individual study to increase teaching effectiveness. A study guide or meeting plan precedes each chapter. Because both viewing and reading are included, you must be the decision maker as to whether the suggested plan is appropriate for you or whether an activity of your own design might better serve your purpose. The chapters in the book and the tapes have been organized in a logical sequence. No one chapter or tape, however, is dependent on your having read or viewed another, so you may decide to mix and match. As long as you have a reason for doing what you're doing, feel free to innovate, but remember that innovation is not good in and of itself without a reason for change.

If you are using this material with a group, usually it is effective to determine a group leader (appointed, elected, or volunteered). That person should have the opportunity to read the chapter and view the videotape before the discussion so she or he can recognize and highlight facilitating contributions from group members and be ready with some examples to prime the pump should the participants have difficulty in generating examples. It also helps to have someone with advance knowledge available, so any misunderstandings or confusion can be cleared.

If as a result of your interaction with the ideas and techniques that are presented you find your teaching is not only more effective but also more satisfying to you and your students, this book and the videotapes will have served their purpose.

About the Authors

Madeline Hunter was Professor in Administration and Teacher Education at the University of California, Los Angeles, as well as Principal of UCLA's laboratory school, now known as the University Elementary School. During her celebrated career, she received the Distinguished Professor Award from the American Association of School Administrators, the Distinguished Service to Education Award from the National Association of Elementary School Principals, and many other honors. In addition to her pioneering work on effective teaching practice, Madeline Hunter also wrote about coaching, motivation, self-discipline, and parent-teacher relations.

Robin Hunter is Principal of Santa Susana Elementary School in Simi Valley, California. He has served as a teacher in a variety of grade levels, as Coordinator of Professional Development for the Ventura County Superintendent of Schools, and has conducted courses in teacher effectiveness for school districts and universities throughout the United States and Canada. Over the course of his career, he has worked closely with Madeline Hunter, both in her publications and in her role as a trainer of teachers and administrators.

**CORWIN
PRESS**

The Corwin Press logo—a raven striding across an open book—represents the union of courage and learning. Corwin Press is committed to improving education for all learners by publishing books and other professional development resources for those serving the field of K–12 education. By providing practical, hands-on materials, Corwin Press continues to carry out the promise of its motto: **"Helping Educators Do Their Work Better."**

Chapter 1

Decisions in Teaching

Guide for Group Discussion or Individual Study

Objectives: *Participants will:*
a. List three categories of decisions in teaching.
b. State generalizations that should be considered in making decisions in each category.
c. Identify their own decisions in each category for a subsequent class.

Anticipatory Set: "If you had to group all the teaching decisions you make in just three categories, what would those categories be?"

1. _____

2. _____

3. _____

Input & Modeling: Read the chapter "Decisions in Teaching."

Checking Understanding & Guided Practice: Teachers must make countless choices daily. Listed here are some of the many decisions teachers may confront. Identify the category of each of the following decisions as one of the following:
1. Content
2. Learning behavior
3. Teaching behavior

Write the number by each statement below, so it can be compared with the answers. When finished, someone might call out "a," "b," "c," and so on, and the group can compare answers by holding up one, two, or three fingers.

The teacher is deciding whether to do the following:
____ a. To read selections from Chaucer or Shakespeare
____ b. To stand by a student to increase that student's concern or move to the other side of the room to lower concern
____ c. To tell students they should not worry if at first things are not clear because everyone has trouble initially

___ d. To have students write a paper or take a test to demonstrate their understanding

___ e. To have students validate their comprehension by making a diorama or a time line

___ f. To have students read the chapter or view a film

___ g. To teach photosynthesis or respiration

___ h. To praise students for what they have accomplished or chide them for what they have not

___ i. To teach by using examples in the book or to create original examples

___ j. To have students learn from discussing or from experimenting

___ k. To indicate the number correct or the number incorrect on a student's paper

___ l. To teach the critical attributes of assumptions and conclusions

Answers

a. 1. Content
b. 3. Teaching behavior
c. 3. Teaching behavior
d. 2. Learning behavior (output)
e. 2. Learning behavior (output)
f. 2. Learning behavior (input)
g. 1. Content
h. 3. Teaching behavior
i. 3. Teaching behavior
j. 2. Learning behavior (input)
k. 3. Teaching behavior
l. 1. Content

Identify the decisions you are making for your next class session as one of the following:

1. Content
2. Learning behavior
3. Teaching behavior

If you are working in a group, check your decisions with another group member. If you are working by yourself, jot them down, so you can inspect them after your class session to see if your predictions materialized.

Independent Practice: Apply this information as you plan for subsequent classes.

Chapter **1**

Decisions in Teaching

Educators have finally arrived at the understanding that professionals in medicine achieved when the latter discovered that germs, and not evil spirits, were the cause of many health problems. We now know of many cause-effect relationships in teaching and learning. As a result, we can use those

"Even champions have coaches."

causal relationships to promote student learning in the same way a doctor uses medical knowledge to promote health. In both education and medicine we are learning more each day even though there still remains much we don't know.

Whenever humans are involved, we are dealing with probability, not certainty. Medication may increase the probability of a patient's recovery, but it does not guarantee it. In the same way, if teachers base their decisions and actions on the principles presented in this book, the probability of student learning will be increased, but it will not be guaranteed.

There is no question that genetic endowment and past experience influence student learning, but your own teaching decisions also have a powerful impact. Consequently, teaching can be defined as a constant stream of professional decisions made before, during, and after interaction with the student; decisions that, when implemented, increase the probability of learning. Students learn more through effective teaching than when they try to learn on their own. Even champions have coaches.

Since the 1960s, educators at the University of California, Los Angeles, have been studying teaching decisions and their implementation—the essence of the teaching process. They found that, regardless of who or what is being taught, all teaching decisions can be placed into three categories:

1. What content to teach next

2. What the student will do to learn and to demonstrate learning has occurred

3. What the teacher will do to facilitate the acquisition of that learning

When professional decisions are made on the basis of sound psychological theory and if those decisions also reflect the teacher's sensitivity to the student and to the situation, learning will be increased. When errors are made in any of those three categories of decisions, student learning can be impeded. Consequently, it is important for teachers to identify consciously and deliberately the decisions they must make in each category and base their decisions on research-validated knowledge. Equally important is the teacher's ability to "read" signals from students and to assess the learning situation, so necessary adjustments can be made.

THE CONTENT DECISION

The first professional decision is to answer the question, "What will I teach?" Perhaps you believe that the decision has already been made. You're to teach honors English, first-grade reading, United States history, advanced placement computer science, fifth-grade mathematics, or French II. However, those subjects merely label the arena in which you will make this decision. In today's world of grade-level content standards, that arena has been even further defined, narrowing the focus of instruction. The content decision referred to here is the answer to the question "What do I teach this group of learners today?"

Dependent and Independent Sequences

Whatever the subject or the content standard within that subject, the answer to "What do I teach?" must reflect your knowledge of what that particular group of students already knows in relation to that content standard and what is next to be learned. This process is very different than having what comes on the next page in the textbook make your determination.

The psychological generalization that guides your decision should be that basic concepts, as well as simple generalizations and processes, must be acquired before more complex learnings can be achieved. Advanced processes and understandings are built on a pyramid of simpler ones.

Brain research identifies this process as building synaptic connections or programs through experience. Students arrive with differing educational

Figure 1.1   Pyramid of Processes and Understandings

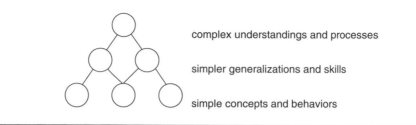

complex understandings and processes

simpler generalizations and skills

simple concepts and behaviors

and life experiences and, as a result, have different connections and programs on which to build new learning. Therefore, to make the decision about the content you are going to teach successfully tomorrow, you need to determine which prior learnings are prerequisite to more complex ones. Make sure those essential learnings have been acquired by your students (not presented to) before introducing advanced material. This is called a dependent curriculum sequence. In this sequence, prior, simpler learning must have occurred before more complex learning can be achieved. For example, a student needs to be able to write sentences before being able to write a paragraph, and write a paragraph prior to writing related paragraphs. The student must have one-to-one correspondence prior to dealing with quantities greater than one. The student must be able to solve for one unknown before solving for more than one. Much of our school curriculum is characterized by dependent sequences.

On the other hand, in some things we teach, the order of acquisition doesn't matter. One can first learn a noun or a verb. One can learn to add first or to subtract first. The Industrial Revolution can be learned prior to the American Revolution. There may be a logical reason for teaching in a certain order, but there is not a psychological reason. This is called an independent sequence: The order of learning doesn't matter. When dealing with a dependent sequence, assessment becomes essential to planning and implementing effective instruction. There is a myriad of assessment tools, ranging from performance assessments to informal, quick assessments used during teaching to determine students' current knowledge and skill levels. It is a waste of valuable instructional time to attempt to teach skills and concepts when there is insufficient prior learning to support the new learning or to teach skills and concepts already possessed by the student.

From Decision to Acquisition

Once the decision has been made about the *what* of teaching, the content decision, teacher and student effort should be directed to the acquisition of that new level of learning, not be dissipated on nonessential or tangential matters. It is tempting to spend class time on vivid or interesting "bird walks" that may distract attention from, rather than enhance understanding of, more important issues. A typical example is, "By the way, that reminds me of something that happened. . . . " If "what happened" will help students understand what is being presented, by all means use the example. If "what happened" is tangential or only loosely related, don't waste time by introducing it. If you have loads of extra time or comic relief needs to be introduced to brighten up the lesson, a bird walk might be forgivable, but most of us find that time and energy are in too short supply to be expended on loosely associated material or random exchanges between students and teachers.

This does not mean you should ignore students' nonrelevant comments. It is a sign of skill in teaching to dignify a student's extraneous contribution without letting it dilute the lesson. "That's an interesting point that will come a little later," usually will handle a tangential contribution. Then do return to it later, either with that student after class or with the group at a time when it is relevant: "Remember when Dylan cited an example of . . . ?"

Don't believe that disciplining yourself with regard to your content decision imposes rigidity on your teaching—it doesn't. Rather, it adds the professional rigor that leads to successful learning. Remember, you're the decision maker. If, during class, a better idea emerges than the one you had planned, by all means, pursue it. Be prepared, but be flexible.

In some cases, you may wish to delegate the content decision to your students and let them decide when they have achieved sufficient mastery to move on. However, as their teacher, you can't delegate your responsibility for the results of that decision and for its potential to increase or interfere with the probability of student learning.

THE DECISION REGARDING STUDENT LEARNING BEHAVIOR

While the first decision of teaching is based on content, the *what* of teaching, the second decision is directed at the student behavior that makes learning possible, the student's *how* of learning. Two important factors affect student learning behavior: input modalities and output modalities.

Input Modalities

Input modalities are the channels through which we get information. Will our students read, discuss, listen, observe, or do? This is the only area in which models of teaching differ: Where does the new information come from? Does new information come from peers, activities, or from the teacher? There is no one best way to learn, and the use of a combination of these sources is usually more effective than relying on only one (see Figure 1.2).

The source of input should be based on the objective (learning outcome) of the lesson. If we want students to develop social interaction skills, we'll probably want them working together rather than listening to a lecture. If the ability to identify similarities and differences is paramount, then an activity requiring them to do so is warranted. If the initial acquisition of a new formula is the focus, a skilled teacher presentation may be most effective. If we want students to develop social skills as well as to interact with the content, we will probably want them working in cooperative groups.

This is why the content decision is so important. What is it that we want the students to learn? The selection of content, and specific learning outcomes from that content, must be the first decision in determining learning behavior that is appropriate to both the content and the learner.

How students get and process information is also affected by their preferred learning style. Some students like to listen, some like to touch, some like to see, some like to talk, and so on. However, all people have many avenues of learning available to them, even if they have a preferred modality. We also know that much modality preference is a result of practice using that modality. The more you use a modality, the better you get at it. Generally, the most effective instruction is that which addresses multiple modalities: instruction where students get to hear, see, touch, and discuss. Again, there is not one best way.

Output Modalities

The second aspect of the teacher's decision about learning behavior is focused on the student's output, which validates the acquisition of the knowledge or skill. That output must be perceivable, so you know—not hope—that one of the following has occurred:

1. The students have achieved mastery and are ready to move on to the next learning.

2. Mastery has not been achieved, and you must reteach or extend practice of the current learning.

Output behaviors that are perceivable and may validate learning include writing, telling, diagramming, solving (so the teacher can see it), reading (aloud), arranging, analyzing (verbally or in writing), evaluating (also so the teacher can see or hear it), and so on (see Figure 1.2). This list is by no means exhaustive, but it illustrates some output behaviors that the teacher can use to assess student learning. This differs from those behaviors that do not validate learning accomplishment. Questions such as "Do you all understand?" or "Do you have any questions?" do not require students to exhibit output behaviors that demonstrate acquisition of knowledge.

Figure 1.2   Examples of Input and Output Modalities

Input Modalities	Output Behaviors
Reading	Reading (aloud)
Listening	Writing
Discussing in groups	Diagramming, solving (so the teacher can see it)
Observing	Arranging
	Analyzing (verbally or in writing)
	Evaluating (so the teacher can see or hear it)

Output cannot be such that the students can bluff, guess, hide, or be lucky in their demonstration of accomplishment. The skilled teacher also gets validating output from a significant number of students—if not all students—not just the one or two who always volunteer. As with the content decision, the input and output student-behavior decision also can be delegated to students, but your responsibility for the results of their decision cannot.

Instructional Objectives

Your instructional objective specifies the first two teaching decisions—(1) content and (2) student learning behavior—and brings both of them to the level of conscious, professional decision making rather than leaving them as vague intentions or wishful thinking.

The following examples make those instructional objective decisions more identifiable. Note that the specific content is capitalized, and the validating student behavior is written in italics. All instructional objectives begin with, "The learner will . . .

The learner will . . .

- *Create* a SPREADSHEET using a computer.
- *Orally decode* words with CVC VOWEL PATTERNS.
- *Create* a T-chart to DETERMINE A FUNCTION.
- *Work in a group* creating a poster demonstrating the WATER CYCLE.
- *Prove in visual space* that πr^2 IS THE AREA OF A CIRCLE (πr^2 is the content but cannot be capitalized).
- *State* the SIX CATEGORIES OF PLANTS and *describe* the CHARACTERISTICS OF EACH.
- *Write* his or her INTERPRETATION OF ARNOLD'S POEM.
- *Answer orally in GERMAN* the QUESTIONS ON PAGE 37.
- *Diagram* the ASSERTIONS AND CONCLUSION.

- *Discuss* the CHANGES THAT RESULTED FROM THE TREATY.
- *Solve* the QUADRATIC EQUATIONS ON PAGE 97.
- *Use* ANAPHORA and EPISTROPHE in an oral speech.

Having an articulated instructional objective, rather than having an intuitive or a subliminal intent, accomplishes two things:

1. It helps you focus your teaching on the learning behavior that you will use to validate whether students have achieved the intended learning.

2. It encourages you to identify the prerequisite learnings that must be taught (and learned) for the students to achieve the intended results.

Objectives and Curriculum

This kind of teaching is essential in an objective or standards-based curriculum, which builds on itself from simpler to more complex learnings. Today's lesson is built on your analysis of the students' work from yesterday's lesson. How the students did yesterday determines what the teacher will have them do today. Are they ready for the next, more complex learning step, or did their output (student work) yesterday indicate that some reteaching or additional practice is necessary before moving on? This type of teaching is much more reliable and predictable in terms of student achievement of those standards than an activity-based curriculum.

An activity-based curriculum is one where students are given a series of activities that are related to the standard. These activities are not related to each other in any systematic fashion and do not necessarily build on each other. What the students will do today does not depend on how they performed yesterday. Clear learning objectives are not articulated nor do the activities build in complexity of demands on the learner.

THE DECISION REGARDING TEACHING BEHAVIOR

The third decision in teaching (note that this is the third decision, not the first) is directed to your own teaching behavior: what you will do to increase learning.

When teachers use learning principles that research indicates are accelerants to student achievement, they can have dramatic effects. Within your power is the ability to increase your students' motivation to learn, the speed and the amount (rate and degree) of their learning, their retention of what they learned, and the appropriate transfer of that learning to new situations requiring creativity, problem solving, and decision making. Principles of learning constitute a powerful pharmacy of alternatives from which you can create an effective learning prescription. Knowing principles of learning and deliberately and artistically using them are the hallmarks of the master teacher. This book was developed to present some of these principles to you and thereby to help you consciously achieve mastery teaching.

"Principles of learning constitute a powerful pharmacy of alternatives from which you can create an effective learning prescription."

The responsibility for making the three decisions of content (what to teach today and tomorrow), learning behavior (what input modalities students are going to use and the student output that will validate successful accomplishment), and your teaching behavior (use of principles of learning to accelerate achievement) sounds like a lot of professional decision making. It is! But in reality you are already making these decisions—purposefully, intuitively, or by default—every day you teach. As you read this book, you will find that you already use much of what is described. However, this book provides you with categories and labels for the decisions you are making and the research that supports them. You may also learn some new techniques that will make your teaching both easier and more successful.

Each chapter in this book focuses on some aspect of professional decision making to help you become more conscious of why you do what you do. As a result, you will become increasingly effective as a teacher.

After you study this book, you will have deliberately constructed a professional launching pad from which your own particular style and artistry in teaching can soar. Bon voyage!

Chapter 2

Increasing Your Students' Motivation:

Part I

Guide for Group Discussion or Individual Study

Objectives: *Participants will:*
a. List techniques they use to increase motivation.
b. Label items on the list according to categories.
c. Generate examples in any neglected category.
d. Try motivational techniques in subsequent classes.

Anticipatory Set: List five to ten things you might do in your classroom to increase students' motivation or intent to learn.

1. _____
2. _____
3. _____
4. _____
5. _____
6. _____
7. _____
8. _____
9. _____
10. _____

Input & Modeling: Read the chapter "Increasing Your Students' Motivation: Part I."

Checking Understanding & Guided Practice: List three factors that affect motivation and give classroom examples of the use of each.

Motivational Factor	What Does It Mean?	Classroom Examples

1. _____

2. _____

3. _____

Examine your original list of items and identify the category as one of the following:

- C: those items that would raise or lower students' level of concern
- P: those items that involve pleasant feeling tones
- N: those items that involve neutral feeling tones
- U: those items that involve unpleasant feeling tones
- S: those items that will increase a student's successful accomplishment

There will be some items that are not discrete; they will fall into several categories. There may be other items that don't seem to fit the categories you have learned about. Don't worry about those (we're introducing neutral feeling tones); you'll learn the labels of additional motivational factors in the next chapter.

If you have no items in any one of the three categories (Concern, Feeling Tone, or Success), this may alert you to the fact that you could be neglecting an important motivational propellant in your classroom. Try to generate some items in that category that you predict might be successful with your students. Compare your items with those of other group members. While each of you has a different teaching style and personality, it is amazing how your repertoire of motivational behaviors can increase as you deliberately incorporate new ideas into your teaching plans.

Independent Practice: Try some new ideas in your class. Some will fit your style or your students' styles better than others. Make sure, however, that you don't narrow your repertoire. Keep adding to it.

Keep your original list because in the next chapter you'll learn to label additional, research-based ways in which you can affect students' motivation to learn.

Chapter 2

Increasing Your Students' Motivation

Part I

M otivation, a student's intent to learn, is one of the most important factors in successful accomplishment. All teachers suffer frustration when a student does not put forth effort to learn. Students may even face us with a stance of "Go ahead and teach; you don't bother me none," a statement made to me by an "unmotivated" student.

It is important for educators to know and believe the following:

- Motivation is not genetic; it is learned.
- What is learned can be taught.
- Teaching is our business.

Therefore, we need to become knowledgeable about, and skilled in the use of, professional techniques that have high potential for increasing student motivation.

Many factors affecting motivation are beyond our control. Students' families, neighborhoods, former teachers, or previous experiences in the same content have all had an effect on the motivation of students in our classes. Currently, we are facing students from increasingly diverse cultural and language backgrounds as well as from nontraditional family structures. Those factors are beyond our control. They have already occurred and are part of students' past.

It's only in the present that we can make changes; thus we need to become skilled in the use of six factors we can modify daily in our classrooms:

1. Level of concern

2. Feeling tone

3. Success

4. Interest

5. Knowledge of results

6. Intrinsic and extrinsic motivation

In this chapter, we will explore level of concern, feeling tone, and success. Chapter 3 takes a closer look at interest, knowledge of results, and intrinsic and extrinsic motivation.

No one of these six factors is most powerful, nor are they completely discrete. They are like the digestive, circulatory, and endocrine systems of the body. There is constant interaction. By adjusting one factor, however, you may restore balance to the entire system.

LEVEL OF CONCERN

One factor you can affect in the classroom is the student's level of concern about achieving the learning. How much does the student care about whether he or she learns? In the past, we believed that stress or concern was undesirable. Now we know that a moderate level of concern is essential to an individual's putting forth effort. If you are satisfied with your appearance, job, or where you live, you will not put forth effort to change it. It is only when you become concerned that you will do something.

For example, when things seem to be going well in your class, what are you motivated to change? Nothing! It is only when you become concerned about new techniques you feel you should learn, or you wish something different to result from your teaching, or another teacher is producing better results, or you are being considered for tenure, or your superior indicates all is not well that you begin to look for ways to increase your instructional effectiveness.

We are seeing a great deal of this in our own professional lives now as the focus on how well students meet district and state standards is brought into high public view. It raises our level of concern about ensuring that all students are successful. As a result, we are motivated to use the most effective teaching skills possible. Should your concern become too high, however, your energy may be diverted from instructional growth to dealing with your concern for self-maintenance or even, at times, survival.

Our teaching decisions are guided by the following psychological generalization: A moderate level of concern stimulates effort to learn. When there is no concern, there is little or no learning. When there is too much concern, there may be no energy available for learning. There are four variables that work to raise or lower level of concern: proximity, time, visibility, and questioning.

Proximity

The closer one is to an authority figure, the higher one's level of concern. Just think about how we react when seeing a police car in our rearview mirror! The further away one is from authority, the lower concern tends to be.

Moving toward a student whose attention is dwindling tends to refocus that student. Seating those students who are most distractible nearer to the teacher has a similar effect. A teacher on his or her feet is worth twenty in their seats because of the ability to rove near to students and see what they are doing.

Time

Level of concern increases when we have time constraints. Have you ever thought in a panic, "I have to be ready for my presentation to the staff tomorrow!"? Time constraints are an effective motivational tool with students, too. If you notice that your students are not showing a high degree of concern about a particular assignment, you might inform them, "I'll come around in three minutes to see how you're progressing" or "You must have your work completed before the break."

On the other hand, when you see that students are overly concerned with what they are working on, such as a difficult new concept or skill, you might want to lower concern by extending time. Some examples of lowering concern include "Why don't you try a problem or two with your partner?" and "Don't worry about finishing them as we'll be working more on these tomorrow."

The exception to the time variable is silence. Long silences tend to raise people's level of concern. You can use silence to your advantage when asking questions, which we'll address later.

Visibility

The more visible you are, the higher your level of concern—witness most people's reaction to public speaking! In many of our classrooms, we have students who remain quietly invisible (and quite possibly mentally disengaged from the lesson or activity) and let the more overt learners carry the participation load. We want all students to put forth effort toward learning. We can greatly increase our chance of success by making all students become more visible during instruction. There are several ways to do this.

Have students raise their hand when they have thought of the answer to your question, but wait for many hands to go up, acknowledging those that are going up with a comment such as, "Good. Several of you are showing me you have an answer, but I'm waiting to see some more hands." Only when you have most of the hands up should you call on someone.

Having students signal their answers both increases their level of concern about participating and, equally important, gives you valuable diagnostic data about how well they understand what you are teaching: "Show me, on your fingers, what number will go in the ten's column" or "Point to the side of the equation where we start to balance it" or "Show me how many syllables you hear in this word." Students can also write their responses on scratch paper or individual lapboards and hold up their answers. All of these methods increase students' visibility and, therefore, their concern to put forth effort into learning.

Questioning

We ask many questions in school and solve many problems. Ideally, every student would answer every question and solve every problem to benefit from the thinking and practice involved. We know, however, that often only one student gets the opportunity to answer a question or solve a problem that has been posed. But, if we stretch our minds a bit, we can get more of our students to put forth effort.

If we have, for example, ten questions to be answered or problems to be solved you can do it in one of two ways: Ten different students can get one practice each or everyone in the class can get ten practices. Which one will yield the most learning?

We want to teach in a way that, as closely as possible, has every student answering every question and solving every problem. Covert learning (thinking of an answer) is as powerful as overt learning (saying the answer aloud). By teaching in a way that activates both of these learning styles, you give more thinking opportunities to all of your students.

But how do we go about doing it?

1. *Beam your question to the group.* Don't name the individual to answer it. In your own class, you can see what happens when you name the student before asking the question. As soon as you say, "Miguel, which

word in this sentence modifies the noun?" all eyes look to Miguel to watch him answer the question. Instead, engage everyone by saying, "All of you find the word in this sentence that modifies the noun." This way all of the students have to be thinking because no one knows who will be asked to answer.

2. *Use wait time before calling for answers.* When we beam the question to the group and then use wait time, two things happen. First, the number of students trying to think of the answer increases. Second, the quality of the answers improves, assuming that the answer requires more than recall. When you ask for students to share their answers, wait for most (if not all) of them to raise their hands. It is fine to call on one student at this point because you know that they have all done some thinking. You can also have students signal an answer, thereby getting additional data about their understanding.

Don't Request Participation—Require It

The words we use when asking questions may also have an effect on our students' level of concern. Being the nice human beings we are, we want things to go well for our students, and, as a result, we are often—unconsciously—not demanding enough. When asking questions, we often plead for an answer or for participation from the group. We hear ourselves asking questions such as the following:

- "Who would like to . . . ?"
- "Could someone please tell us . . . ?"
- "Could we have a volunteer to come up and . . . ?"
- We know that "Not me" is the response silently uttered in many students' minds. Instead of pleading with students to participate, expect it. Phrasing your questions in the form of directives sends a very different message. Here are some examples of instructions that engage student thinking: "Everyone find with your eyes the item that doesn't fit the category. I'll know you've got it when you are looking at me."
- "Think of what you'll say when I ask you to reexplain why you invert the divisor when multiplying fractions."
- "Be ready to explain what balance in trade means."

Each of these instructions carries a message of high expectation that all brains need to be in gear.

A hallmark of predictably effective teachers is that they consciously and deliberately raise or lower the concern of the group (or individual) when a change in level of concern is needed to increase effort. In looking at the class and seeing students on task, attentive and responsive, there is little need for the teacher to do anything, as student concern is causing effort toward learning. If that is not the case, however, then the previously discussed variables can be used to increase or decrease concern.

FEELING TONE

One of the major findings of recent brain research is that the human brain is an emotional structure, not a logical one. The way students feel in a particular situation affects the amount of effort they are willing to put forth to learn. Feelings exist on a continuum that extends from pleasant → neutral (no feelings associated) → unpleasant. Obviously, students are most inclined to put forth effort to learn if they find the learning situation pleasant. In addition, if they believe that they will be successful learners (which creates a pleasant feeling), they are more apt to try.

"An awareness of the three feeling tones and facility in creating each of them, when needed, are the hallmarks of a teacher who is proactive on students' motivation rather than merely being reactive to their lack of it."

Pleasant Feeling Tones

Common sense as well as research would tell us to make our classroom environment a pleasant one where students have a high probability of achieving success. We can accomplish this in a number of ways.

*Make Your Students Feel Personally
Important or Significant in the Classroom*

Recognizing that the brain is an emotional structure, we know that the relationship between teacher and student is tremendously important. When conducting staff development, I frequently show a videotape of an eighth-grade science class, which begins during the passing period. The students are trickling in and moving to their seats while the teacher is at the door. I turn the video off just before the period begins, and I ask the group of teachers, "What can you tell about this class before any instruction even begins?" Their response is invariably that "the students like being there." This is because the teacher is at the door greeting and briefly talking to the students as individuals. There exists a good relationship, which the teacher nourishes daily.

Use Humor Wisely and Effectively

The use of humor in the classroom can be a powerful tool in facilitating pleasant feeling tone. Appropriate use of humor, without it distracting from the learning, not only builds great feeling tone but also the desire to be there and the desire to put forth effort.

Celebrate Your Students' Efforts

A room adorned with excellent student work honors individual and group accomplishment and communicates high standards—not to mention excellent models. Likewise, the teacher who appropriately acknowledges productive behavior throughout the day makes the class a pleasant place to learn.

All of these efforts by the teacher foster a sense of community and create an atmosphere where students feel safe to learn. This book was designed to assist you to accomplish this very objective.

Unpleasant Feeling Tones

Unpleasant feeling tones also activate a learner to put forth effort: "If that isn't finished, there will be undesirable consequences." Most of us are reluctant to use unpleasant feeling tones in our classrooms. The reason is that, although unpleasant feeling tones are effective in stimulating effort, the effort they generate is not entirely directed toward learning.

Humans learn best in an environment that is absent of threat, where all of the brain's neural energy is used to accomplish the new learning. When threatened, much of that energy is redirected toward survival, to get out of the situation that is causing the unpleasant feeling. In schools, students may not be physically threatened in the classroom, but they may feel threatened by humiliation or loss of dignity, which can have the same negative effect on learning.

Unpleasant feelings can also have undesirable side effects if they remain unpleasant. The student may learn but also may avoid that content area or teacher in the future. Each of us has had the experience of learning something with unpleasant feeling tone (a burn from a stove while cooking, Latin conjugations, English grammar, statistics, etc.). We got through the ordeal, and we may still remember what we learned, but we have avoided that situation or content ever since.

While we need to be aware of and occasionally use the power of unpleasant feeling tones (when pleasant ones aren't working), we should strive to eliminate the possible aftereffect of student avoidance by returning to pleasant feeling tones as soon as students put forth effort to learn (see Figure 2.1).

Neutral feeling tones, neither pleasant nor unpleasant, are void of motivational propulsion. Neutral feelings are useful, however, to

Figure 2.1 From Unpleasant to Pleasant: Reward Effort With Encouraging Commentary

- "I've really put a lot of pressure on you, and you've responded magnificently."
- "In spite of your struggle with these concepts, you've emerged with a clear understanding of them."
- "I know you were unhappy about the demands being made on you, but you should be proud of the improvement in your performance."
- "Many of you have felt discouraged and wanted to give up, but your perseverance has paid off."

Figure 2.2 Use Neutral Feeling Tones to Reassure Students

- "Everyone is tired and confused, so let's forget it today and work on it at another time when we're fresh."
- "Don't worry if you missed several; it won't count on your grade, and you now know what you need to study."
- "This is our first attempt, so don't be concerned if you don't understand. We'll need to do several before it will be clear to you."

terminate an unproductive or unpleasant situation so that, later, we can return to the task with pleasant feelings (see Figure 2.2).

Your professional task is to determine whether it would be more productive, in terms of students' intent to put forth learning effort, for them to experience pleasant, unpleasant, or neutral feeling tones. No one feeling is always the most productive. An awareness of the three feeling tones and facility in creating each of them, when needed, are the hallmarks of a teacher who is proactive on students' motivation rather than merely being reactive to their lack of it.

SUCCESS

A third factor that increases students' motivation is the feeling of success. To feel successful, one must expend effort and have a certain degree of uncertainty about the outcome. We do not feel successful when we put forth little effort for accomplishment. If we turn the knob and the door opens, we feel no elation. We knew what would happen. If the door is jammed and, by exerting skill and effort, we manage to open it, we feel successful.

It is the same with learning. If the task is easy and requires little effort, we feel little success and are not motivated to continue. If, with effort and with no guarantee we can accomplish the learning, we achieve it, we feel successful and usually are motivated to try to do more.

You may wonder how you can affect students' successful achievement. Isn't it a result of the students' ability and effort? In part, yes. But student success is also responsive to two other factors within your control. The first factor is the level of difficulty of the learning task. Because you determine and assign the task, you can adjust the level of difficulty at any time. The second factor is your teaching skill. It's no great mystery that the most able teachers achieve the highest levels of student learning success. This book aims to increase your skill in the deliberate use of elements that make you an increasingly effective teacher.

Know When to Raise and Lower the Academic Bar

Try to think of successful achievement in terms of clearing an intellectual high jump bar. A high jump can be made easier or more difficult as the bar is lowered or raised. For the Olympic champion, it should be set just above the level where success is reasonably predictable. Clearing the bar is not certain; it will require effort. The champion will be challenged to try and will feel successful as it is cleared. If the bar is set too low, and the champion bothers to perform the jump, there will be no feeling of success because there was certainty of clearing the bar. Champions don't continue to jump a bar that anyone can get over.

On the other hand, short-legged, stubby Kenny won't even make an attempt if the bar is set high. He's sure he can't clear it, so he's unmotivated to try. If the bar is lowered to the point where he thinks he has a reasonable chance of clearing it, he may be motivated to attempt it. As he experiences success, the bar can be raised, and, with skilled coaching to improve his jumping techniques, he'll continue his effort.

This raising or lowering of the bar is very much under the control of the teacher. We all have grade-level achievement standards that students are expected to attain. Our first task as teachers, however, is to see where the students are in relation to those standards. Where does their prior knowledge leave off and new learning need to begin? This questioning stems from the psychological premise that many learnings are incremental; that is, more complex learnings are built on attainment of simpler learnings.

If our standard is to write a five-paragraph expository composition, we need to see what the students have already learned toward that end. Are they able to write a paragraph? Related paragraphs? Introductory or concluding paragraphs? This is why assessment is so important: to find out what the students already know and can do so that subsequent instruction is at an appropriate level of difficulty. If the learner perceives that the learning task is of little or overwhelming difficulty, there will be little motivation to expend the effort for it.

Know How to Assess Individual Student Readiness for Learning

The analytic ability to take complex standards and break them down into their component learnings is a valuable one for the teacher to develop, both from the perspective of looking at where students are in relation to attaining the standard and in being able to work with students who are having difficulty and need additional assistance. This is a very different type of teaching (having the assessment process drive subsequent teaching) than presenting what arrives on the next page in the book, regardless of what the students know or how they did on the previous page. The professional educator uses textbooks as tools for specific instructional purposes. Textbooks should not be the determiners of what is taught or when it is taught. Only the teacher knows what the students already know, what they are ready to learn next, and what type of learning activities will have the highest probability of being effective.

The more success students have experienced in the past, the more optimistic they are about future performance. Even if there is a greater risk of failure, students with previous experiences of success will be apt to try. Studies on student engagement rates indicate that an appropriate instructional level is one where the students are correct in their responses about 75% of the time. This success rate leads to high task engagement. However, this is for students who have experienced success in similar situations in the past.

On the other hand, the more students have failed in the past, the less willing they are to expose themselves to risk because their prediction is that they won't make it. Therefore, to protect themselves, they won't try. They are unmotivated. For these students, our at-risk students, we need to build in smaller learning steps that give a success rate of 95–99% for them to continue to expend effort.

Consequently, we need to lower the academic bar for less able students. This does not mean we let them get by with less but that we build in the support and assistance needed, so they can clear that educational bar and try for the next higher one. As a quick illustration, your class may have read a story or chapter in the textbook, and you are now discussing it with them to assess their understanding and to further develop the ideas presented. So that all students experience success, you might begin with recall- and comprehension-level questions, where there is a high probability that all students can answer. Then build to more challenging questions (application, analysis, etc.) that push the top students. At this point, since all students have now heard the answers presented, the students who answered the initial questions can now be pushed to paraphrase the answers to the more challenging questions—a demanding but less risky task.

If the curricular standard is, for example, to have all students succeed in writing a paragraph, and if you have several students who still struggle with writing related sentences, then you know that is the skill you teach before moving on; they will never write a paragraph without accomplishing that skill. On the other end, students who have mastered writing a paragraph can be pushed further by working on more sophisticated skills, such as varied sentence structure or multiple paragraphs.

The same holds true for reading. For students to gain automaticity in reading with comprehension, they need text levels that allow about 95% successful decoding when reading. If the text is more difficult, then comprehension and the development of automaticity suffer. When we look at our class of learners, it may be necessary to work with flexible small groups. By giving more concentrated attention to students, we can establish an effective program in any curricular area where subsequent learning is based on successful achievement of prior learnings.

Differentiate Your Instruction

Teachers of elementary, middle, high school, and university students are learning to raise and lower the academic bar and tailor instruction to different learning needs in the same class in a variety of ways. One way for teachers to differentiate instruction is to work directly with some smaller groups in class, flexibly grouped for specific learning needs and heterogeneously grouped for cooperative learning tasks (something that is very common in elementary schools where the students have much less ability to work independently), while having other groups work independently of the teacher (see Chapter 17, "Teaching for Independent Learning"). Working with smaller, flexible groups within a class enables the teacher to give additional help and to raise and lower task difficulty to meet different student needs, thereby using the factor of successful accomplishment to increase students' motivation to learn.

THE INTERACTION OF MOTIVATIONAL FACTORS

Again, no one factor—concern, feeling tone, or success—is most important. Each interacts with the others, and we use them in concert. If there is some risk but not too much, the student experiences mild concern. When that student is successful, pleasant feeling tones result.

As you consciously use a stimulating level of concern (enough to get students to put forth effort but not so much that it diverts energy), as you deliberately create pleasant feeling tones (if they do not work, you may need to use slightly unpleasant ones and, after the student is energized, return to pleasant), and as your teaching makes success as a result of effort not only possible but probable, you will exert a major influence on your students' motivation to learn.

In the next chapter, you will learn three additional factors that you can adjust to affect students' motivation to learn.

Chapter 3

Increasing Your Students' Motivation:

Part II

Guide for Group Discussion or Individual Study

Objectives:	*Participants will:* a. State three additional elements they can change in their classrooms to increase students' motivation to learn, and generate examples of each. b. Experiment in subsequent teaching with all six possibilities for increasing students' motivation to learn and then select for future use those that appear to be most effective.
Anticipatory Set:	Recall Figure 2.1, where you listed three ways to increase students' motivation (intent to learn). Look at your original list of things you might do in your class and locate the items you couldn't label.
Input & Modeling:	Read the chapter "Increasing Your Students' Motivation: Part II."
Checking Understanding & Guided Practice:	List the three additional elements (Interest, Knowledge of Results, and Extrinsic-Intrinsic Motivation) and generate examples of each that could be effective with your students. Examine your next teaching objective and generate techniques in each of the six categories of motivation that you might use in your next class session. You probably won't use all of them, but this activity will give you the opportunity of selecting from a repertoire of alternatives those you predict will be most effective. This type of decision making is the essence of the process of teaching.
Independent Practice:	In your next class, try the techniques you selected. The reactions of the students will help you further refine your effectiveness in influencing students' efforts to learn. All of us tend to get in a rut and repeat what has worked for us in the past. Occasionally, you may want to go back and reread the two chapters on motivation so you can take advantage of the full repertoire of motivational possibilities, rather than majoring in only a few.

Chapter 3

Increasing Your Students' Motivation

Part II

In Chapter 2, you learned about three factors affecting student motivation that the teacher can control: Level of Concern, Feeling Tone, and Success. This chapter will identify three additional factors: Interest, Knowledge of Results, and Intrinsic-Extrinsic Motivation. Remember that no one factor is most important and often they work in concert. By changing only one or two factors, however, we can make a tremendous difference in students' intent to learn.

INTEREST

The fourth factor that has been demonstrated to affect a student's intention to learn is interest in the learning task. Interest is not inborn; it is acquired. The teacher can promote interest in several ways.

Use Students' Interest in Themselves

There is no one more interesting to you than you. There are several ways in which a creative teacher can make material more interesting (see Box 3.1):

- Use students' names in positive examples.
- Relate the material to be learned to students' lives.
- Use examples that refer to students' experiences in the class.
- Make positive statements about students' performance or their learning effort.

Box 3.1   Make It Personal: Teacher Commentary to Get Students Interested

"You will be writing a persuasive letter to your parents, convincing them to increase your allowance. What are some of their concerns that you would need to address?"

"John, suppose you were presenting an argument for electing your friend Jeffrey, and Charles wished to challenge his position . . . "

"If we were to increase the percentage of A's in this class by . . . "

"Notice that Angela has the pigmentation most commonly associated with Nordic races, while Sue's is more typical of Latinos."

Increase the Authenticity of the Task

An activity is authentic when it has a high level of meaning for the students or is directly related to their lives, either inside or outside of school. Brain research shows that we learn very quickly and efficiently that which makes sense to learn. By teaching the skills students need to master while they are doing an authentic task—something we would do in the world outside of school—interest in the learning increases (see Box 3.2).

Box 3.2   Examples of Authentic Tasks for Students

- Learning measurement in the process of building book cubbies for storing personal belongings in the class.
- Learning Internet and communication skills while having the students research the best prices for transportation and accommodation for an overnight study trip.
- Learning effective communication skills by writing the principal or superintendent asking for a playground or campus improvement.

Not only does authenticity increase interest in the learning, but it also facilitates the actual learning itself.

Vary Your Practice

A third way we can make material more meaningful is by accentuating the novel or vivid: that which is different or unexpected. We can achieve novelty in our classrooms by such simple devices as the following:

- A change in your voice and movement around the classroom, making your students follow where you're going, physically and instructionally.
- A change from lecturing to questioning.
- Lesson plans that involve teacher-directed instruction as well as discussion and activity in cooperative work groups (if appropriate to your objective).
- Use of the Internet. If you're reading *Pride and Prejudice,* have your class research the Regency period online to better understand the mores of Jane Austen's time.
- A film or video. If your class is studying the Civil War, you could finish the unit by showing the highly acclaimed film *Glory* (of course, adhering to copyright laws!). Film and video can be used effectively as a teaching tool or as a sedative. Be sure you know the difference.

Anything different from what is usually experienced can elicit an alerting reflex in the student's brain and greater attention results.

Nothing continues to remain different, however, because habituation results and the student may no longer be attracted to the new thing. Consequently, we must take advantage of the alerting reflex to teach, so the material begins to have value on its own merit, not because it's presented in an entertaining way. Just a little variety usually will do the trick of eliciting attention. Too much vividness or flamboyance can actually distract from the learning.

Demonstrate That the Material Itself Is Novel

Your students should have more interest in what you present when the material is something they don't expect. Try promising them a surprise or surprising them with your introduction:

- "The property that makes a fungus different from every other plant is that, like a human, it cannot manufacture its own food but must get it from some other source."
- "Let's look at the validity of these two assertions: (1) Students who don't study always get better grades, and (2) the more boring the book, the easier it is to remember."
- "The results of this experiment will really surprise you."

Using novelty may also increase the motivational aspects of the practice that students do.

Skills such as developing fluency with numbers, math facts, phonics skills, or vocabulary require practice (see the chapter on designing effective practice) to reach automaticity. Embedding these skills in game formats brings novelty and motivation to the necessary practice whether used alone, with a partner, or in a group. Brief sponge activities (activities that productively use short bits of time to practice) as students come into the room, as well as transitioning between activities or during clean-up, also use novelty to bring increased interest to practice.

A combination of novelty and relating the learning to the student will capture students' interest and therefore increase their motivation to learn (see Box 3.3).

Box 3.3   Sparking Interest to Increase Motivation

- "When you order your favorite McDonald's milkshake, it won't melt even if you heat it in the oven. That's the result of an emulsifier made from the algae we're studying."
- "Suppose you believed in reincarnation. In your next life, what would you need to accomplish what you didn't accomplish satisfactorily in this life?"
- "You are going to make up your own test. Ask three questions that you believe would really check a person's understanding of the chapter and then answer them. Your grade will reflect the quality of your questions as well as the answers."
- "Discuss three important skills you need to develop to make you a more effective group member, leader, friend, writer, reader, or class officer."

Almost everything we teach can be related to something in the student's own life, thereby making that content more interesting. Even if there is no novelty in the content itself, the *way* we present it, *what* the students do with it, and *how* they let us know they have learned it can be different from mundane expectations in classrooms, which hold little novelty—only more of the same.

A caution needs to be sounded so we don't make things so novel or vivid that

"Use novelty and vividness to attract students' attention to learning, not to distract from the learning."

students focus only on the novelty and not on the content. Students (and sometimes we) can get so intrigued by the novelty, we forget the reason it was introduced in the first place: to increase students' motivation to learn that which was not novel. Madeline Hunter reported witnessing one teacher demonstrating part-whole relationships with a luscious cake. Students' minds were so engaged with the final disposition of the cake (wishfully, in their stomachs) that they missed the fractional understandings of the lesson.

KNOWLEDGE OF RESULTS

A fifth and very powerful element we can change in our classrooms is the amount, specificity, and immediacy of the feedback students receive about their performance: their knowledge of results.

Simply performing a task, without knowing how well we did it, is not very satisfying or stimulating. As a result, we are not motivated to continue or improve our performance. We are motivated to try to accomplish improvement when we find out the following:

- What we are doing well
- What needs to be improved
- What to do to improve it

When students feel that reasonable probability to improve exists, then they are motivated to try and accomplish that improvement. Grades usually are neither immediate nor specific enough to give knowledge of results that actually motivate. Witness the river of discarded papers as students leave school each day! An *A* or *B* simply informs the student, "Don't worry; you're doing OK." The student, however, does not know which part was OK or whether one part was superb and other parts need to be improved.

Focus on Feedback

Motivation, the intent to put forth effort, will increase if the student has specific knowledge of results. Feedback such as "Your ideas are excellent. Now you need to give examples of how they would look if implemented," encourages students to carry their inspiration into application. Telling a student, "You seem to know the content, but you need to organize it into sequential relationships. For example, you might . . . " stimulates the student to organize and categorize. "Your use of examples is superb; now you need to draw generalizations from them" encourages students to move from specifics to conclusions. Each of these comments has infinitely more motivational potential than an *A* or a *B* grade.

It takes more time to put comments on a student's paper than it does to write that terminal grade. Therefore, to save your time and energy and to increase your own motivation to convey knowledge of results in your classes, use class participation with immediate feedback plus frequent, brief tests and papers for students' responses (see the chapter on checking students' understanding). A one-page (or less) essay not only requires students to tighten their thinking (they can't "run off at the pen"), but it also enables you to go quickly over a set of class papers and return them with immediate and specific knowledge of results. As a result, students will be motivated to improve their thinking, as well as the product of that thinking.

Use Rubrics

The use of rubrics is an excellent way to provide students with the knowledge of how they are performing. Rubrics find function not only in the initial stages of a project or task to provide specification as to what qualities/skills need to be demonstrated, but they can also be used to evaluate the resulting product. The more specific the rubric is in delineating the characteristics of different levels of performance, the more effective it is in providing instructional feedback to the student (as well as instructional direction to the teacher).

Beam Questions

Your students also can receive knowledge of results as you beam a question to the whole class, give them several answers from which they choose (a verbal multiple choice situation), and then give them the correct answer with the reason it is correct. This teaching technique gives knowledge of results with no public humiliation for those who were incorrect and gives a feeling of success plus pleasant feeling tones to those who responded correctly. Remember that it is a teacher decision-making model. Techniques (and the principles that guide them) are neither good nor bad but more or less effective given the conditions and intent for which they are used.

Provide Feedback Effectively

We tend to think of only one source of knowledge of results in the classroom: the teacher. While teachers are a powerful source of feedback, their time is heavily impacted by assessing, teaching, reteaching, planning, and analyzing student work, as well as a multitude of demands outside of the classroom. When time is limited (as it is), what feedback should the teacher spend time giving?

The teacher has unique skills and knowledge that can be used to help students acquire new skills and concepts. Generally, then, the teacher should spend his or her time giving knowledge of results on new learning. It is when the student is attempting new skills that the teacher's expertise is most effectively used in guiding the student's efforts. Teachers' skills should be used to assess what students do well, the areas in which there is room for improvement, and—most important—how to modify their teaching.

By circulating during the initial practice and giving feedback on the first few problems, sentences, letters, and so on, the teacher can very quickly give knowledge of results at the most critical time—in the initial attempt at new learning. Providing verbal feedback on students' publicly shared answers not only presents knowledge of results to the student who shared but also lets the others hear and compare what they thought with the teacher's response.

In longer, more involved student projects (such as reports, compositions, or science projects), the teacher can provide knowledge of results on parts of the project so that the students can modify and improve along the way. By the time the project is completed, the quality is undoubtedly higher as a result.

When giving individual students feedback on their writing during a writing conference, have a couple of other students who are next in line sit and listen; it benefits them, too. It is also the responsibility of the teacher to give a grade on final tests and completed, long-term, complex projects after students have had the benefit of specific and immediate knowledge of the results of their work during the initial stages of learning.

Offer Alternate Sources of Feedback

There are many things students do in school that do not involve new learning. These are activities that students already know how to do and are doing for practice to increase speed, accuracy, or facility with the skills required. In these situations the teacher doesn't need to be the source of knowledge of results. Three alternate sources of feedback are discussed in the following sections.

Materials

Many activities require checking for accuracy of math problems, punctuation, answers to questions, and so on. In these cases, materials can be provided for the students to self-correct their work, which gives them immediate knowledge of results. Frequently giving them the direction to do the first four and then check with the answer key before doing the rest, for example, lets them know immediately how they are doing and allows for the opportunity to change anything before proceeding. By doing an effective job of teaching, we have already gotten evidence that they can do work fairly accurately, or we wouldn't have had them practice independently.

Peers

When students work together, they can provide necessary knowledge of results to each other. When teaching writing and focusing on a particular attribute or skill, have the students bring their work to Read Around Groups (composed of three to four peers). This not only lets them read their work and receive feedback from their peers but also gives the peers additional reinforcement of the skill by looking for it in several other pieces of writing. At the beginning of a class period, have students partner up and compare answers in their homework. If they agree, then it's probably correct. If they disagree, then encourage them to discuss it until they come to agreement.

Self

Providing the students with, and having them use, rubrics is a very effective way to have them self-evaluate their work. Rubrics can range from the very simple ones used in kindergarten and first grade (having students make sure they put their name on the paper, used proper punctuation, and spaced words appropriately) to very sophisticated rubrics for complex projects in the upper grades. Student involvement in the assessment of their work is powerful in helping them see the efficacy of their efforts and, as a result, increases their motivation to continue to put forth effort into their learning. When excellent performance has been modeled and accompanied by rubrics specifying the attributes of different levels of performance, the students—applying them to their own work—can see the next learning step in improving the quality of their products. This places the student at the center of the learning process with ownership of that process, as opposed to having to solely rely on outside feedback to set improvement direction. It also correlates success with effort, the only attribute that the student has total control over.

Encourage Diversity of Thinking

While we do need, and are motivated by, quality feedback, there are times during which we do not want to validate students' answers as to their correctness. Sometimes, we want a free flow of thinking regardless of the correctness of the responses or when there are may be many avenues to the answer and we want them all explored.

In mathematics, for example, we may get a student's response to solving a problem and say, "Tell me how you arrived there. How did you think about that? Can you tell us . . . ? Did anyone have a different way of approaching the problem?" In this way, without validating the correctness of anyone's answer, you are encouraging diversity of thinking. We are also providing the student with multiple examples of how other students are thinking about the topic.

INTRINSIC-EXTRINSIC MOTIVATION

No doubt, as you read about these five motivational factors that every teacher can change in the classroom (level of concern, feeling tones, success, interest, and knowledge of results), you are wondering what happened to intrinsic motivation: students supplying their own propulsion to learn. If students were always intrinsically motivated and showed up in our class pleading, "Teach me. I'm ready!" we could forget everything in this chapter. Unfortunately, this usually is not the case.

Intrinsic and extrinsic motivation exist as opposite ends of a continuum, which represents the relationship of the learning to the goal achieved. Completely intrinsic motivation exists when satisfaction from the activity is the student's primary goal. The student does something to enjoy the activity, simply doing it. When students learn to achieve some result from having accomplished that learning (earning an *A*, getting the course over with, meeting a requirement, becoming knowledgeable in that content), they operate from more extrinsic motivation.

Intrinsic motivation is not necessarily saintly, nor is extrinsic motivation sinful. Both are effective. The difference is that with intrinsic motivation you are doing something because you wish to do it. Satisfaction comes from engaging in the learning process. The more you learn, the more satisfaction you receive, and the more you want to learn. Consequently, intrinsic motivation is self-perpetuating. Hobbies and games (when winning is not the objective) are typical examples of activities in which the players are often intrinsically motivated; that is, where the process rather than the product is the primary goal.

When you exert effort because of extrinsic motivation, once the goal is achieved (you passed the course, you finished the paper, you took the test), you no longer have the goal as an extrinsic motivator. As a result, effort ceases. However, suppose that while you were putting forth effort, you were (1) somewhat concerned about the outcome, yet you experienced (2) the pleasant feeling tone of being (3) successful. Your success made the material seem more (4) interesting, novel, and related to your own life. In addition, your teacher gave you (5) immediate and specific knowledge of results about what you had accomplished and helped you to continue to improve your performance. There is a high probability that you enjoyed the whole process and your motivation moved from the completely extrinsic toward the intrinsic end of the continuum. Now you are more motivated to do it some more because you enjoyed it for the intrinsic satisfaction of the process rather than the extrinsic goal.

Many of us are concerned because our students are extrinsically motivated. It is important to remember that a great deal of what each of us does every day is also extrinsically motivated. We get up, go to work, hand in reports, grade papers, take inservice classes, and read books such as this one not because we find intrinsic pleasure in each of these activities but because they enable us to achieve the goal of being an increasingly competent professional. If we find that the pursuit of teaching excellence becomes an exciting and rewarding pastime, we'll become more intrinsically motivated to reread this book and seek other sources continually to increase our instructional effectiveness.

One result of efforts to learn about motivation is increased awareness of factors that increase students' motivation. We change from intuitive or random use to deliberate inclusion of six motivational factors in teaching: to move students from completely extrinsic motivation (they have to learn it) to more intrinsic motivation (they enjoy learning it). The increased learning dividends for students guarantee escalating intrinsic motivation for our own professional growth.

Chapter 4

Getting Students Set to Learn

Guide for Group Discussion or Individual Study

Objectives:

Participants will:
a. State three ways to use prime learning time in their classes.
b. Generate activities that are productive in terms of student learning and can be used during class administrative chores.
c. Generate activities that will develop productive anticipatory sets for subsequent class periods.

Anticipatory Set:

Respond to these questions:
1. How important to students' learning are the first few minutes of class? Explain your answer.
2. As a result of your belief, what advice would you give to teachers regarding those first few minutes?

Input & Modeling:

Read the chapter "Getting Students Set to Learn."

Checking for Understanding & Guided Practice:

Review your answers to the two questions in the Anticipatory Set and reexamine your initial responses.

Generate a list of activities you could use in your class while handling administrative or housekeeping matters. (Notice that each study guide in this series begins with an anticipatory set, and you are given the objectives of each chapter.)

Identify the objective for your next class. Generate some anticipatory sets that might be used to focus students on the learning, give them some practice that would help them accomplish it, and give you some diagnostic information about their entry knowledge.

Determine how you will let students know the objective of your next class and why it is important for them to achieve it.

Independent Practice:

Try out your ideas in class. Remember, even if these techniques are not new to you, consciously thinking about them may be. As a result, you may not be as fluent or comfortable using them initially as you will once these teaching techniques become automatic.

Chapter 4

Getting Students Set to Learn

HOOKING YOUR STUDENTS' INTEREST DURING PRIME TIME

First impressions are important, and the beginning of your class or lesson is no exception. You have certainly experienced how important first impressions of people or places can be. Research in learning validates that effect. Information introduced at the beginning of any sequence is more easily learned and better remembered than equally difficult material encountered later in that same sequence. This generalization is true, all other factors being equal, regardless of whether the sequence is a list of words, a group of concepts or generalizations, the pages of a chapter, the class period, or a week or a month of instruction. The beginning of any class or lesson is the prime time for that

> *"students usually will expend more effort and consequently increase their learning if they know what it is they will learn today and why it is important to them."*

learning. Obviously, when certain material is more vivid, more meaningful, or more interesting, it will be more easily learned and remembered regardless of its position in a sequence.

We need to take advantage of the learning propulsion inherent in the beginning of our class and not waste that beginning prime time on soap opera activity. Prime time can be wasted while we wait for the stragglers to arrive, take roll, collect or pass out papers, correct homework that isn't essential to today's lesson, make announcements that aren't that important or don't have to be made in prime time, or engage in other "administrivia." Such activities often are better placed later in the period when they won't burn up powerful beginning time. If something other than today's content must be taken care of at the beginning of class, it can be combined with important learning activities.

Using Prime Learning Time Effectively

Handle nonlearning business in the classroom while getting students to review concepts and techniques they have recently learned.

Direct a Review Question to the Entire Class

Take part of the roll or pass out papers while all students are thinking about the answer to the review question you've posed. Call on a student whom you anticipate will give the correct answer. Then ask another question and use students' thinking time to continue your housekeeping or class keeping chores. By using beginning time in this way, each student has the opportunity—and the obligation—of formulating an individual answer and then checking what is heard against what was thought. Correction of unvoiced misunderstandings or erroneous answers can be accomplished without visibility or embarrassment.

Ask Students to Write Something Independently

For example, have students define a few vocabulary words in their own words, write a short summary of the generalizations taught the previous day, or solve a math problem that will provide a discussion entry to today's lesson.

Journaling. Frequently, teachers have students keep a journal in which they write at the beginning of the day or class period. If this is the case, have a focus to the writing. Whatever the topic, even if it is a free write, have the students focus on a writing skill. For example, instruct them to work on writing a good topic sentence, to use variety in their sentence structure, to be descriptive, to pay attention to smooth transitions or appropriate letter spacing. Giving focus ensures that this teaching down time serves as a short practice of those skills we want the students to internalize.

Summarizing. Brain research shows that having students summarize or paraphrase information is effective in helping move material into long-term memory. Using prime time at the beginning of the period or class to have students write a brief summary of the key ideas discussed or read the previous day is time well spent both in remembering and in resurfacing the ideas on which you will build today.

Reviewing the Basics

Students can always benefit from practice to internalize the basics, such as math facts, spelling, vocabulary, or sight words. During this beginning time, students can work in pairs, quizzing each other on these essential skills. What kinds of skills do your students need to practice? Using this prime time for short practices yields learning dividends and gives you several minutes to handle administrative or class keeping chores.

Giving Feedback

Feedback to the students on their work can be quick, teacher-provided answers, or you can have students share their answers with the class or a partner. Whether or not the work done during this time is collected is up to the discretion of the teacher. When having students summarize, however, you should tell them the key ideas they should have included, giving them knowledge of results, so they have the opportunity to verify or correct their thinking immediately.

Anticipatory Set

Even when you have to sacrifice some beginning prime time to other functions, you should take advantage of the beginning of your class to create an anticipatory set that will take your students' minds off of other things and focus their attention on that day's content. An anticipatory set is an activity that brings mental focus (activates the neural programs necessary) to the upcoming learning activity. An anticipatory set may hook into and bring forward students' past knowledge and experiences, which facilitates the acquisition of that day's learning. An anticipatory set may also provide valuable diagnostic information about the knowledge or skills the students already possess, their cognitive, affective, or psychomotor entry behavior.

Student entry behavior (which is prerequisite to achievement of the new learning) is what students already know and can do and how quickly and effectively this information and skill will help them achieve the new learning. Entry behavior is usually a better gauge of speed of acquisition of the new learning than is IQ. Consequently, entry behavior constitutes important diagnostic and predictive information for a teacher. This information often can be gathered by an anticipatory set.

Anticipatory Sets: Some Examples

1. Imagine that you're told you will learn the five types of poetic feet. You probably would take your mind off other things and concentrate on what you knew or could remember about poetic meter ("Let's see, there was something about iambic and dactylic . . . "). Your answer to this challenge could indicate your degree of sophistication in that area and give you practice in recalling what you knew. You would also hear the answers of other people with more (or less) information than you. As a result, you would be more focused on a lesson on iambic pentameter than you would be if someone just began teaching it without first capturing your attention. In addition, the teacher would have an idea of where to begin your instruction.

2. Have your students explain why cucumbers and okra could legitimately be served in an all-fruit salad. Such a question would surely focus them on consideration of the critical attribute that determines whether something is a fruit or a vegetable and encourage recall of what they already know in that area. Their answers to the assignment would reveal information important to you in the development of the subsequent lesson.

3. Instruct your students to write a sentence with a dependent clause preceding an independent clause, and another sentence with the independent clause coming first, and to punctuate both sentences correctly. This activity focuses students on dependent and independent clauses and gets them thinking about which sentence requires a comma. It also gives the teacher examples created by students from which the class can subsequently work, something that is usually more interesting and, therefore, more motivating than using only teacher-generated examples. If the teacher circulates around the room, glancing at papers in the few minutes that students are writing, diagnostic information about the level of students' knowledge is immediately available (with no papers to take home and correct—a dividend in itself!). Even if not all papers are examined, representative samples will supply valid information.

4. Provide students with a few decimals and common fractions and ask them to put them in order from smallest to largest, with an explanation of how they went about their decision making. This not only activates their "fractions programs" for the upcoming lesson but also gives you a glimpse of their understanding of the concepts.

5. Get primary reading students thinking by asking them to think of, and be ready to tell, a problem encountered by the main character in a story they read the previous day. Or have the students read to themselves initially, then have them read out loud a list of words, applying the phonics skills they had been working on (if that was your objective).

The variety of effective anticipatory sets is limited only by your creativity and by how precisely you map out the objective of the current day's class or lesson.

Objective

Your instructional objective is another important aspect in using prime time at the beginning of your class. Students usually will expend more effort and consequently increase their learning if they know what it is they will learn today and why it is important to them. It is seldom that what we teach has no relevance to a student's life, but frequently students do not make the connection. Consequently, in most (not all) cases, the students will benefit if you tell them the day's objective and the purpose or reason for that learning.

Box 4.1   Examples of Setting Objective and Purpose

"From our work today, you will know how to analyze poetry you don't understand, so its meaning becomes clearer to you."

"Today, we'll clear up any confusion you might have about the use of commas. It will save you a great deal of time because then you'll know for sure that your report is correctly punctuated without having constantly to check rules."

"Today, you'll learn about calorie intake, so you can regulate your weight while eating foods you enjoy."

"You're going to learn the classification system of animals, so you'll better understand their similarities and differences."

"After today, you'll be able to determine when conclusions are valid and when they're not. That's a skill you can use when you want to argue for a change in the rules at school, at home, or in an organization to which you belong."

"Authors use different techniques to hook the reader. Today, you'll learn three of these techniques, so people will want to read what you've written."

"Today, you'll learn how to compare the cost of various types of interest rates, so you'll always know which will cost you the least, regardless of the advertisement."

If you decide that you want your students to figure out the lesson's objective or its relevance on their own, that is fine. Just be sure that when you don't tell students in advance what they will learn, that is what you intend, rather than having the omission result from your forgetting to do it. The true loss occurs when teachers do not realize the potential learning accelerant from telling students the day's objective. Research shows that learning is dramatically increased when students know what they are supposed to learn and why it is important to them.

Again, it is your decision whether or not you tell students the objective or learning outcome from their effort. At times, telling them can be the wrong thing to do. Regardless of what you do or don't say, certainly you should know exactly what learning outcomes you are trying to achieve. As a result, you'll be able to ascertain, with evidence, that the students have achieved the outcomes and you can move on, or that they have not yet achieved them, and you must go back and reteach.

CULTIVATING PRIME LEARNING

In summary, we can take advantage of prime time at the beginning of our class when we do the following:

- Give students something to think about, recall, or practice if there is wait time before class can start.
- Use an anticipatory set that will focus students on the content to be learned. In addition, anticipatory sets can give diagnostic evidence of the entry behavior of the students and serve as activities that facilitate the acquisition of new learning. If, after deliberation, you decide not to have an anticipatory set for a particular class, that's all right. But if absence of an anticipatory set is not the result of deliberation but of default, that's not all right.
- After students have cleared their minds of irrelevant things and are focused on the present lesson, motivation to learn and increased effectiveness in learning can be achieved by letting the students know the objective (intended learning) and why it is important (unless you wish them to discover it or be surprised).

Using prime time in these three ways should facilitate your students' ability to be ready for the information, process, skill, or activity that you have designed to help them achieve the objective. How to plan for that part of your class and how to carry out your plans effectively are the subjects of the next chapter.

Chapter 5

Providing Information Effectively

Guide for Group Discussion or Individual Study

Objectives: *Participants will:*
a. Identify three principles that increase the effectiveness of giving information.
b. Organize information for a subsequent class according to these principles.
c. Generate a plan for how that information will be presented to students and identify the examples to be used.

Anticipatory Set: List some of the principles that guide you in the process of giving information to your class.

Input & Modeling: Read the chapter "Providing Information Effectively."

Checking for Understanding & Guided Practice: List three principles that increase the effectiveness of giving information.

Complete the following tasks using the content of the next information-giving session you will teach:
a. Specify the information essential to students' understanding. Select an organizational design (temporal, cause effect, simple to complex, relationships of categories, etc.) and organize the basic information.
b. Practice giving some of the information in simple language with unambiguous examples. Try this out with other teachers of different content areas. If they can understand your presentation, you can be sure your students will.
c. If possible, design a model that students can experience directly.
d. Examine the printed and visual materials you are using in your class to see if they adhere to the three principles.

Independent Practice: Teach your planned information session to the class. Observe carefully for student reactions that will give you feedback as to which techniques were successful and which need further modification.

Chapter 5

Providing Information Effectively

Information constitutes the foundation for learning and thinking. Without information we can't think, make decisions, solve problems, or be creative. Once we have adequate information, we can proceed to build concepts, develop generalizations, and engage in higher level thinking.

There are many ways to acquire information, and there is no one best way. In addition to direct experience, students can use the valuable, vicarious experiences provided by books, films, discussions, and lectures.

Writers and producers of audiovisual material provide information that has had the advantage of much time and great care in preparation and editing. Once completed, however, all adjustments must be made by the teacher or the learner, or both, to speed up, slow down, skip, reread, or stop to consider. Also, the writer or filmmaker must prepare the information for anonymous learners, not knowing whether the examples are meaningful for a particular group of learners, whether the message is understood, or whether it needs to be expanded or requires modification.

Lectures have bad reputations. Maybe you're familiar with the sayings "telling is not teaching" and "the sage on the stage." Chinese proverbs tell us that "What I hear, I forget" and popular wall charts read "I remember 5% of what I hear, 10% of what I see." All of these sayings condemn us to using any modality other than telling. This is nonsense. It depends on *what* you tell and *how* you tell it.

Some very effective learning occurs from listening. In addition, social knowledge, of which students learn a great deal in school, can only be transmitted by telling. On the other hand, some learning, such as procedural and problem-solving knowledge, is gained through experience, most effectively through well-guided experience. We can all think of many important things we've gained from only being told and shown. I recently had the experience of being taken sailing. Wanting to assist, I was told and shown what to do, the theory behind the actions I was to perform, and how sails and wind direction interact. Had I been left to my own devices to figure this out, I would probably still be drifting aimlessly in the Pacific.

Make Sure to Modify

Poorly designed lectures certainly do not teach effectively. A well-designed lecture, however, can be adjusted to each learner's needs in terms of examples used, pacing vocabulary, and idea density. A lecture also can be modified on the basis of signals given during the lecture by students, indicating their confusion, lack of interest, need for additional examples, or need for the relief afforded by humor. As a result, the lecturer has the advantage of being able to adjust the message as it is being delivered: to say it in a different way, to give personalized examples, to include a humorous episode, or to increase or decrease the demands on the students who are listening. The critical element of a lecture is to diagnose the amount of information students can process before they must interact with it. After the teacher makes the diagnosis and instructs accordingly, students are able to integrate new knowledge with the knowledge they already possess, enabling them to move it into long-term memory, so they can retain it for use in the future.

Educate From Expertise

Because so much teaching is done directly, this chapter focuses on that method of delivering information. However, this model of instruction is not a direct instruction model but rather a teacher decision-making model. Much of the curriculum targeted at each grade level is new learning for the students. It often involves new vocabulary, concepts, and processes. Often this type of information is most efficiently and accurately presented by someone (usually the teacher) who knows the material and knows how to sequence, demonstrate, and assess students' understanding of the material and relate it to their experience and knowledge.

Once students learn the information, to move to an application level, they have to use it. This enables them to develop meaning, learn strategies, and see patterns and applications. This level of learning comes through well-designed activities that engage the students with the material and each other. These activities can be done individually, with a partner, or in cooperative groups. They can be, but are not limited to, experiments, discovery activities, or creative application of concepts or generalizations. These activities must be appropriate for both the subject matter and the students. But first students must have the information with which to perform the activities.

THREE PRINCIPLES OF EFFECTIVE INSTRUCTION

Regardless of the content or message, adherence to three basic principles will help you to communicate information more effectively. These same principles also apply to preparation of written or audiovisual materials.

1. Determine Basic Information and Organize It

First, we must determine which information is basic or essential to students' understanding of the content or process and then separate that information from information that may be desirable but is supplementary and can be acquired later. That basic information must be organized, so it becomes the scaffolding, or advance organizer, to which students can add more complex information. For example, in understanding the contribution of NASA's *Apollo 11* moon landing in 1969, it is basic that students know the political climate of the time; what the voyage meant for technological advancement; what happened before, during, and after the voyage; and the changes that resulted from the journey. Basic information needs to be organized, so it constitutes a tapestry of related information rather than a patchwork of bits of information.

There is no one best way to organize information. Categories for organization may be temporal, cause-effect, or topical, such as beliefs of the times, personality characteristics of those involved, or dangers of the voyage. The organization selected should not only reflect the needs and interests of the students but also promote acquisition, comprehension, and retention of the relationships within the material or process being learned.

Box 5.1   Temporal Organization: An Example

Energy comes from the sun. That energy is absorbed by plants and enables them to use elements from the soil to manufacture food. This process is called photosynthesis. Animals eat plants and, with oxygen from the air, are able to convert them to energy. This process is called cellular respiration.

Once students have perceived the basic relationships inherent in photosynthesis and respiration, they are able to add more complex information.

Organization facilitates understanding and retention. The research has shown that when information is organized, the retention of that information increases rather dramatically. Research also shows that it doesn't matter whether the teacher or the student organizes the information. Either way the effect is the same. In many cases, the teacher, having greater mastery of the content, would be the one to provide the organizational structure. In some cases, however, having the students

> *"Basic information must be organized, so it becomes the scaffolding . . . to which students can add more complex information."*

(where appropriate) provide their own organizational structure is very beneficial to learning and remembering.

All information, regardless of the subject matter you teach, should be examined for basic structure and presented to students in an organized way. As a result, students will have the foundation of concepts and generalizations on which to build more involved understandings.

2. Present Basic Information in the Simplest and Clearest Form

Once we have determined the information basic to students' understanding, and then organized it so students see the relationship of the parts to each other and to the whole, we need to present that information in the simplest, clearest, and most understandable way. We should use words we are sure the students understand, and accompany concepts and generalizations with examples that are unambiguous and that highlight the essence of the information we present.

For example, in describing Columbus's sailors' fear of falling off the edge of the earth, the teacher might use the example, "Suppose you were riding in a car on a dark road where there was a bridge that you had heard was washed out. The driver of the car believed the bridge was intact and was proceeding at a great rate of speed. How would you feel riding in that car, approaching the area where the bridge was supposed to be? That's the way many of the members of Columbus's crew felt as they imagined they were approaching the edge of the world."

Get in Your Students' Heads

What do these concepts look like from your students' lives? If the concepts are initially presented in a meaningful manner (as they relate to the students' past experience), they are more easily understood in the context of the content area you are teaching.

For example, in the late 1800s, the American economy was in an inflationary spiral. Under these conditions, people in debt had the opportunity to benefit. Such was the case of the American farmer, who was most likely a debtor. In teaching the relationship between inflation and debt, the teacher might ask the class, "Do any of you drive cars to school but have your parents foot the bill for it?" You'll probably see several nodding heads. The teacher can proceed with, "Let's say that your car was purchased for $15,000, and your parents are making payments of $300 per month on that debt. Now, because of inflation, the same car would cost $18,000 to purchase. Your parents would still be paying $15,000 for what is now worth $18,000. Likewise, American farmers, in debt for land and machinery, benefited from the escalation of the value of their property as they were still paying on the *un*inflated value."

In mathematics, presenting concepts through activities that allow the students to focus on and recognize the meaning (rather than being overwhelmed by algorithms full of large numbers) builds a quicker and more thorough understanding of, and ability to use, these concepts. It is this generalization of teaching something in its simplest and clearest form that has students working with concrete materials to build understanding before moving to symbolic or abstract relationships.

Teach Generalizations Before Exceptions

Of course, exceptions exist to almost every generalization. While it may be appropriate to state to your students "this is not always the case," it is wise to introduce only exemplars at the beginning of instruction. Leave exceptions for a later time and introduce them only after students understand the concept, generalization, or process in its simplest form. It is perfectly legitimate to instruct your students with the following generalizations:

- "Plants must have light, water, and chemicals to manufacture food. Animals must have animal or plant food, water, and air to manufacture energy."
- "Suppose you and a plant were in a beautiful sunny garden with an automatic sprinkling system. The plant would thrive, you would get hungrier and hungrier, and, if there were no plants you could eat, eventually you would die. Suppose on the other hand, you and the plant, without its roots in soil, were in a sunny, well-stocked kitchen. You would thrive; the plant would die."

At this point, it's best not to introduce information about plants that are parasites and, therefore, do not manufacture their own food.

The science and art of citing examples is so important in teaching that Chapter 8, "Making Material Meaningful," will help you develop skill in selecting and using examples that increase your students' learning and retention of the information you teach.

3. Model the Information or Process

Finally, if at all possible, we need to model what we mean by demonstrating a process or showing a product that elicits a response from the students such as "Oh, I see!" or "Now I understand what that means." Modeling is so critical to learning that it is the subject of Chapter 7, "Modeling What You Mean."

Model Unfamiliar Concepts

If students have already experienced and can visualize in their minds the concept or generalization being taught, a model—something tangible you can perceive in the classroom—may not be necessary. It would be silly to blindfold students and have them walk near the edge of something high. They already have experienced that feeling and can recall it. With photosynthesis, on the other hand, it might make the concept more vivid if students perceived the growth of four plants: one without elements from the soil, another without water, a third without light, and a fourth with all three of the elements necessary for photosynthesis to occur.

Using the same generalization of presenting information in the clearest and simplest way, your models should clearly illustrate the concept you are teaching. When teaching how to write topic sentences, for example, be sure that the examples you use are very clear in their statement of a generalization that the detail sentences support.

Save Student Models for Later Learning

Having students provide the models in the initial stages of instruction can muddy the waters of new learning. Remember that the initial stages of learning are extremely powerful and you want the students to see clear, accurate examples of the concepts being taught. I have seen teachers fishing for examples from the students, usually throwing several back before catching a good one. By the time the students see or hear a quality example, they've already heard several inaccurate ones dramatically diluting the power of a good example. Ensuring that your models and your examples are unambiguous and demonstrate vividly and validly the principle or process you are teaching yields powerful learning dividends. Introduce exceptions only after the students solidly understand the concept in its primary, unambiguous form. For example, use a plant that does not manufacture food only after students understand photosynthesis and are ready for exceptions.

TAKING THE STEPS TO SUCCESS

Let's see if we have practiced what we are preaching about giving information. Our advance organizer was, whenever information is being given, whether it be by lecture or prepared materials, you need to keep three basic principles in mind:

1. Information that is basic to students' understanding must be identified and organized so that it constitutes a scaffolding, or advance organizer, to enable students to see the relationship of each part to other parts and to the whole.

2. Information must be presented in language that is clear and unambiguous to the students, with examples that highlight the essence of the concept or generalization.

3. If appropriate, a tangible model should be used, so students can directly perceive the process or product.

I also attempted to explain, in simple language, what was meant by each of those three principles, using verbal examples. Finally, I hope that what you are reading serves as a model of the process of giving information I am attempting to convey to you.

Each of these *Mastery Teaching* chapters was developed to constitute a model of giving written, auditory, and visual information (note that I say a model of, not the way). When the academic content area you must teach is unfamiliar to you, I hope the advance organizer will enable you to apply basic information to your own content and help you to incorporate the techniques presented here in your daily teaching.

Chapter 6

Teaching to Both Halves of the Brain

Guide for Group Discussion or Individual Study

Objectives:	*Participants will:* a. Recall four principles for using chalkboards or other visuals. b. Examine prepared visuals to determine if they should be augmented by chalkboard use. c. Design visual use that spatially demonstrates the relationship of ideas or concepts for subsequent classes.
Anticipatory Set:	List some principles that should guide a teacher's use of visuals.
Input & Modeling:	Read the chapter "Teaching to Both Halves of the Brain."
Checking for Understanding & Guided Practice:	List four principles of chalkboard use. Identify a concept or relationship in your own content and design a way you could demonstrate that relationship with visuals. Examine prepared visuals you commonly use and determine whether or not introducing them with simple diagrams would facilitate students' understanding.
Independent Practice:	Try these instructional techniques in your next class.

Chapter **6**

Teaching to Both Halves of the Brain

Do you believe a picture is worth a thousand words? If your answer is "yes," you're right—part of the time. If your answer is "no," you're also right—part of the time. When a choice is to be made, which do you use: words or pictures? Most of the time, you need to use both, so students have an opportunity to do integrated brain processing of information.

YOUR BRAIN: THE LEFT AND RIGHT OF IT

The Left Hemisphere

Brain research shows that most people process information sequentially in the left hemisphere. You are probably using your left hemisphere as you read these words. You add what you're now reading to what you just read a moment ago. You also will carry those ideas forward into what you read in the next paragraph. You are building bridges of understanding sequentially across time. Your left hemisphere is a temporal, analytical, if-then, sequential processor.

"In the same way that you will catch more balls if you use both hands, you will catch more ideas and information if you use both hemispheres."

The Right Hemisphere

You would be using your right hemisphere if you could see my posture, facial expression, my pauses to think, and my general demeanor as I write. If you were listening to me speak, you would also use your right hemisphere to process additional information from my body language; from the tone, emphasis, and juncture of my speech; and from any visuals I might use to illustrate meaning. With your right hemisphere, you could see what I meant. It is no accident that we use the expressions "I see what you mean," "in my mind's eye," and "Oh, I see!" The right hemisphere is the mind's eye: It processes information that is perceived simultaneously and derives meaning from visuals, nonlanguage sound, or position and relationships in space.

Integrating Hemispheres

Your right and left hemispheres are connected by a heavy band of nerve fibers, the corpus callosum, which enables those hemispheres to work together, to cross-talk. Neither hemisphere is more powerful than the other. You need them both. In the same way that you will catch more balls if you use both hands, you will catch more ideas and information if you use both hemispheres. Consequently, in teaching, we need to direct information to both hemispheres so that a student is not restricted to only right or left hemispheric input. This way, students achieve integrated-brained learning, thereby eliminating much lame-brained learning.

Although the evidence to support integrated hemispheric processing is relatively recent, teachers have been aware of the value of chalkboards, overhead projectors, and, most recently, computer screens since these devices first appeared in schools. Unfortunately, because teachers didn't know the reasons why visuals were important to learning and how visual information gets processed, these tools often were not used as effectively as they could be. In addition, now that complex visual aides have become available, they also are used without discrimination, with the illusion that the more real, the better. Figuratively speaking, we sometimes make the error of bringing an elephant into the classroom to teach the concept gray and wonder why everyone is distracted.

Clearly what is needed is not only an awareness of right hemispheric processing but also a set of discriminators that helps teachers determine the conditions under which the simplicity of a chalkboard or overhead projector is effective and conditions when more complex visual media are preferable.

USING VISUALS TO FACILITATE LEARNING

In this chapter, we're going to divide visuals into two categories: emerging visuals and static visuals. Emerging visuals are visual assists that are created, or emerge, as instruction proceeds. For example, let's say a teacher starts a lesson with a blank chalkboard, chart, or overhead transparency. As the lesson progresses, new points or diagrams are recorded, and, as a result, visuals emerge as the lesson unfolds. This same concept is what one sees in PowerPoint presentations, even though the visuals are prepared in advance. To the learner or audience, the visuals are emerging as new material congruent with the progress of the presentation or lesson.

Static visuals are those that do not change throughout the lesson. Prepared transparencies, posters, photographs, objects (realia), or prepared chalkboards all fall into this category.

Emerging Visuals

One guiding generalization for learning is at the beginning of learning, present information in its simplest form. This would indicate that, in many (not all) cases, the use of emerging visuals is warranted during initial stages of instruction. In this way, the teacher controls the amount and nature of the information being presented. However, there is more to emerging visuals than knowing this simple generalization. When we use an emerging visual, we need to keep four basic principles in mind.

1. Say Before Writing

The first principle is based on three assumptions:

- We can say something faster than we can write it. Consequently, when we say it, the learner can immediately begin processing the information in the left hemisphere and does not have to wait until meaning begins to emerge from the words being written.
- The learner does not have to guess the meaning, possibly erroneously, while trying to complete the not-yet-finished message as it is being written.
- The silence that occurs while the message is being written on the chalkboard provides the three to eight seconds needed for the information to go from initial perception of the words or message to storage in short-term memory. When one message or idea is followed immediately by another, it is possible for the second idea to eradicate the first. A few seconds of silence enables the learner to store a message in the short-term memory bank for later retrieval.

This principle also applies to PowerPoint presentations. When you say something aloud, the learner initially hears the complete message and then watches it emerge once more while reading what you have just said. When done the other way around, often the learner is busy reading and does not attend to what you are saying. Remember the power of visuals. What you see is what you believe. We have learned that what we see is usually more important, since someone took the time and effort to write it out. If information is up on the board or screen, it means that it is important, and that is what students attend to. Witness the college class with an overhead filled with an outline of the day's topic. While the professor lectures, the students busily copy the outline, ignoring the lecture. Say it first. Then write it or have it emerge.

Consequently, most (but not all) of the time we say what we are going to write on the chalkboard before writing it. Obviously, if for some reason we wish the learner to see an unknown message emerge or attempt to guess the complete message as it appears, we write without stating what we are going to write.

2. Use Key Words and Simple Diagrams

It is important that the learner focus on the key concepts or the central ideas of what is being presented. While we may elaborate on these concepts or ideas in speech, on the chalkboard those ideas should stand out and not be lost in clutter. The greater number of items there are in visual space, the less important each becomes. Art museums usually hang one painting on a surface so that it stands out in high relief. In an arrangement of paintings, each becomes less noticeable. Generally, you will remember the image of a single painting far longer than you will remember any one in an arranged group.

Consequently, we write as few words as possible. If we use a diagram, we make it simple. By doing so, we make it possible for the student's right hemisphere to process what is seen, while the left hemisphere processes the elaboration provided by your words. The integration of those two functions should contribute to more effective learning and retention. For example, while we say, "On your chalkboard, use key words and simple diagrams," we write "key words—simple diagrams."

3. Position = Relationship

The use of visual space provides the opportunity to indicate relationships of concepts and ideas through their position in that space, a relationship that can be processed in the student's right hemisphere. An outline is an excellent example of position in space indicating relationships. Look at the following outline:

I. Use of Visuals

    a. Use of emergent visuals
    b. Use of static visuals

The position of A and B indicate they are parallel ideas, both of which are subsets of, but not as inclusive or important as, Roman numeral I. The position in space of the items in an outline provides important visual input to help clarify the relationship of ideas.

If we write on the chalkboard

Washington
Jefferson,

we imply that Washington comes first in some order (election, to be studied, discussed, etc.).

If we write

Washington Jefferson,

we imply there is parallel or oppositional relationship, not a first, second relationship (unless we number them). Arrows, lines, and simple diagrams all indicate (to the right hemisphere) the relationship of the items in visual space. Another example where position indicates relationship is frequently seen in prewriting webs, in which teachers and students generate a nonlinear outline of the organization of ideas for their writing. Helping students position information when note taking (by our use of it when presenting information) provides powerful right hemispheric assistance for when they are studying at home.

When we are aware of the power of spatial positioning on relationships, we avoid placing items on the chalkboard, chart, overhead transparency, or PowerPoint presentation in a haphazard fashion or simply where there happens to be space. As a result, we place each item deliberately, so its position indicates its relationship to other material on the chalkboard (causal, oppositional, numerical, temporal, comparative, categorical, etc.).

4. Erase Before a New Concept

In the same way that a clear head encourages clear thinking, a clean board encourages effective learning. The final principle that guides emerging visual use is to erase everything that is not necessary before proceeding to the next idea. Erasing holes in the information on the visual so that bits and pieces of previous ideas are left, writing between other ideas, and using every inch of space all constitute right hemispheric atrocities because what you are presenting gets lost in the visual competition for attention.

Sometimes, teachers do not erase because they do not want to waste the time necessary to clean a board. They are wise to realize that each precious minute should be spent on learning. However, a simple solution to that dilemma is to give the students something to think about or to do that enhances learning while you are erasing. For example, you could make the following statements:

- "Be ready to tell me the four principles of chalkboard use."
- "Be ready to state in one sentence what you consider to be an important facet of Washington's personality."
- "Write down your own definition of the word."

This technique will stimulate the students to review what has been learned, hold them accountable for evidence of that learning, and give you time to clean the board, so the next idea is just as clear visually as it is in your verbal presentation.

Static Visuals

There are times, of course, when the simplicity of the emerging visuals is not as effective as is the motivational impact or the time saved by use of static visuals. Neither emerging nor static visuals are good in and of themselves; it's how they are used and for what purpose that determines their effectiveness.

Sometimes you will want to have an outline or elaboration of your content already prepared on an overhead transparency. This is fine, provided you keep in mind that students will begin copying instead of listening to you. To prevent this, show them the entire overhead, so they see the sequence of the content to be covered. After a brief period of time, take a piece of paper and cover all but the initial concept, generalization, or information you want them to focus on. Explain the information; then uncover it on the transparency. Allow time for students to copy the information, and, when you see their eyes return to you, you can begin to discuss the point, giving examples and explanations.

When using photographs, posters, static charts, or realia, first let the students take in the visual as a whole because often the whole gives the learning the necessary meaning. After they see the whole, focus them (through words, covering, or pointing) on that to which you want them to pay particular attention.

As the teacher, you must decide whether the simplicity of basic information presented verbally and accompanied by simple visuals on a chalkboard will better promote learning or whether the vividness, accuracy, and reality provided by realia, pictures, tapes, and motion pictures will be more motivating and enabling to successful learning. Just remember that when you use the easily accessible chalkboard or overhead, your use should reflect awareness of the following principles:

1. Say before writing.

2. Use key words and simple diagrams.

3. Position = relationship.

4. Erase before new concept.

Obviously, say before writing and erase before a new concept do not apply in the same sense to many static visuals, such as photographs and realia. They do, however, apply to static linguistic visuals where, once the students have seen the whole visual, you will cover that which is not needed at the time. Inevitably, your left-brained, right-brained, and no-longer-lame-brained learners will profit.

Chapter 7

Modeling What You Mean

Guide for Group Discussion or Individual Study

Objectives: *Participants will:*
a. State four characteristics of an effective model.
b. Develop models in their own content area that display those characteristics.
c. Incorporate models in subsequent instruction.

Anticipatory Set:
a. Explain the difference between a model and an example.
b. List the characteristics that make a model effective.

Input & Modeling: Read the chapter "Modeling What You Mean."

Checking for Understanding & Guided Practice:
a. Identify the four characteristics of an effective model.
b. Examine models used in your classroom to see if they possess those characteristics.
c. Devise new models that will augment or improve on those used in the past.
d. Share your models with other participants for analysis.

Independent Practice: Continue to develop and analyze models used in subsequent classes and devise ways of improving them.

Chapter 7

Modeling What You Mean

"Give me an example" is a common request we hear when some-one does not understand what is meant. A model is one kind of example, one that a student can perceive directly in the classroom, rather than having to rely on the memory of some previous learning or experience. A model may be concrete, such as a model of the human heart or a model of a miniature city. A model may be a replication, such as a picture, or a symbol, such as a diagram or map. Finally, a model may be verbal (written or spoken), such as a paragraph, a sonnet, or an alliteration.

"Oh, I see" or "I see what you mean" are words that usually indicate the learner has processed a perception and assigned significance, which is deeper than perception. For example, a teacher might see students looking out the window, doodling, yawning, or slumping in their seats. The assigning of significance to that perception is indicated by the teacher's reaction and response, "I see you think this information isn't important, so let me show you with some examples how it influences your life."

FOUR CHARACTERISTICS OF EFFECTIVE MODELS

Seeing, hearing, or feeling a model of what is meant can become a tremen-dous assist to understanding. "I see (or hear, or feel, or taste, or smell) what you mean" can result if the models used by the teacher have four important characteristics.

1. Effective Models Highlight the Essential Combinations of Attributes

One characteristic of an effective model is that it highlights (and the teacher labels) the critical attribute (or attributes) that distinguishes what it is from other similar things. Unless critical attributes are obvious, identified, and labeled, students' attention can be attracted to or distracted by irrelevant characteristics, resulting in uncertainty or confusion.

Consequently, it is important that a model be carefully chosen to make sure it presents the concept or generalizations in an unambiguous way. Generating a model while teaching

> *"Thinking on your seat is easier than thinking on your feet."*

can be a burst of brilliance, but more often the spontaneous model is not as clear as it could be and results in confusion. Usually models should be developed or selected in advance.

"Peter Piper picked a peck of pickled peppers" is a more obvious model of alliteration than "the plowman homeward plods his weary way." A cow is a better model of a mammal than is a whale.

Working first with a simple model of the heart, with the chambers, valves, arteries, and veins clearly marked, makes later identification of those same parts in a real heart easier and also makes for a good example, where novelty and vividness do not distract from what you want the students to learn.

2. Models Avoid Controversial Issues

In selecting a model, it is wise to avoid controversial issues, which can arouse emotions and divert learners' attention from what is being taught. Current political issues may make for interest-arousing models; however, they can also distract the learner's attention from the critical attribute of the model and center the focus on the pros and cons of an issue. Consider the following examples:

Model of the use of *is being*.

"The taxing of luxury products is being considered" versus "the taxing of fast foods is being considered for health reasons."

Model of the use of *its* versus *their*.

"Each party considers its platform to be the best" versus "the Democratic Party considers its platform to be the best."

3. First Models Must be Accurate and Unambiguous

The beginning phase of any learning is critical to successful achievement. Errors introduced in this prime time are more difficult to eradicate those that occur later in the learning sequence. Consequently, first models must be accurate, which is something that is not as likely if students generate the initial models. A well-thought-out model presents the concept as clearly as possible. Later, students can generate models to demonstrate that they understand and can apply what is being learned.

4. Models Eventually Introduce Nonexemplars

Half of knowing what something is is knowing what it is not. After you have presented several carefully selected, unambiguous models without emotional overtones and your students have demonstrated understanding, you may wish to go in a new direction with the information. Present models to your class that require students to make discriminations based on the presence or absence of the critical attributes they have learned. The decision to introduce more ambiguous models is based on your judgment that students are ready for more complex discriminations and no longer need models that clearly highlight the critical attribute.

MODELING PROCESSES, PRODUCTS, AND EXAMPLES

Modeling as exemplified here refers to processes (how to go about something), products (what the end result of the completed task looks like), and examples (to help students see what you mean). For some examples of how models can be used to better understand concepts, see Table 7.1.

Other models may be used to help students learn processes such as dancing, playing a game, solving a math problem, or completing a thought process that moves from beginning to end. Then, there are models that involve a process that results in a product. Writing an expository composition, creating a spreadsheet, creating a T-chart, painting a watercolor, or cooking a recipe illustrate this category.

An important dimension in planning for modeling during a lesson is to decide if students need to experience only a process, only a product, or a process that results in a product. This helps us determine what we need to teach. If we want the students to understand how to read a spreadsheet, our modeling is focused on that task. However, if we want the students to understand how to read and create a spreadsheet, then an additional type of modeling is necessary. If we want the students to be able to interpret the data from an experiment, we should provide models that allow them to do that. If, in addition, the ability to design an experiment is a goal, then the

Table 7.1   Modeling for Understanding

Model	Concept
A cutaway engine	Helps students understand the parts involved and how they work together to move air and fuel through the engine to create power
A business pricing a product	Illustrates the idea of supply and demand
A spreadsheet	Assists students in understanding how information may be displayed in an organized manner for easy retrieval

modeling of that process is called for. Students' ability to see and understand something may be very different from their ability to create it. Depending on the learning we want the students to accomplish, we must be aware of and select different, appropriate models to build into our instruction.

MODELING YOUR THINKING

Another frequently overlooked but powerful type of modeling is the thinking required to accomplish a task. When students are faced with a new, complex learning task, modeling the thinking an adult does in approaching the task is very helpful. In teaching analysis-level thinking skills where students must compare and contrast, the teacher can model how to do it. Consider the following examples:

> "In trying to identify likenesses and differences in the two characters, the first thing I'm going to do is decide what categories I'll use to compare them. I could use temperament, family context, interests, their approach to problem solving . . . "

> "Here is how I usually look for the main idea of a passage."

> "Here's what I think about when I write a good transitional sentence."

In this way, students who may have no idea how to approach the task have a process modeled for them. I have experienced confusion in a statistics class, while watching immense equations emerge and wondering, "How in the world did the professor get there?" To adults who are very familiar with the content, knowing how to go through a task takes little thought. However, familiarity can hinder our teaching as we attempt to approach it from the unfamiliar perspective of a new learner.

As we learn something new and get more facile with it, we internalize it to the point of automaticity and forget the learning steps we went through when we first learned it. Make sure you are able to articulate how you go about a task so that others who don't know can benefit from this modeling of thought processes. Such models can be very illuminating.

Sometimes, it's not possible to provide a visual or verbal model that students can benefit from in the classroom. In this case, we encourage students to reach into their memory bank of knowledge and experience to supply meaning for the current learning. In the next chapter, I discuss the use of this technique to make material meaningful.

Chapter 8

Making Material Meaningful

Guide for Group Discussion or Individual Study

Objectives: *Participants will:*
a. Identify four methods of making material meaningful.
b. List six principles to guide the selection of examples from students' past experience to add meaning to current learning.
c. Generate examples that embody those six principles using the content of a subsequent class.
d. Design a mnemonic device to be used with content that previously has presented problems.

Anticipatory Set: What is meaning and why is it important for learning?

Input & Modeling: Read the chapter "Making Material Meaningful."

Checking for Understanding: List the four methods of making material meaningful. List six principles that guide the choice of examples.

Guided Practice: Given your content, generate an example of how you could use each of the four categories to make that content more meaningful.

Independent Practice: Try these instructional techniques in your next class.

Chapter **8**

Making Material Meaningful

Meaning is one of the most important propellants of learning. Meaning, however, does not exist in material but in the relationship of that material to students' past knowledge and experience.

In Chapter 7, you learned to help students generate meaning for students by using models. Models are examples that the student can directly perceive in the classroom. We could create a model of the relationship of present learning to past experience and to future learning using the following diagram:

Past knowledge and experience → Present learning to be acquired → Future situations to which learning is to be transferred.

The student can perceive in visual space the relationship of past, present, and future learning.

While it is possible to provide models of speech, actions, excellent paragraphs, diagrams of interactions, or physical models of reality, often it isn't possible for students to perceive directly many of the concepts and generalizations we teach. Consequently, we need to become skilled in the use of four additional techniques that help students generate meaning in material.

FOUR TECHNIQUES THAT MAKE MATERIAL MEANINGFUL

1. Use Examples From Students' Past Experience

We increase students' ability to generate meaning in material when we use an example from students' past experience. Such an example prompts students to reach back into their memory banks and bring previous knowledge or experience forward. As a result, acquisition of new learning accelerates and that learning becomes more meaningful.

The words we use in examples convey meaning only to the extent that they elicit from learners' past experience the concepts that are relevant to the present situation. For example, to a child the word *balloon* elicits the concept of a plaything or something you might see at a party or carnival. To a balloonist, the same word elicits a very different concept. Using examples of sentences with those words, such as "We use colorful balloons at children's parties" and "*Around the World in Eighty Days* is the story of a balloon flight," clarifies which meaning is intended. In addition, previous learning is brought forward to increase accuracy of meaning and accelerate acquisition of new learning.

To use examples successfully, teachers can follow six basic principles:

Identify the critical attribute(s) of the present learning.

Select from students' own lives some previous knowledge or experience that exemplifies the same critical attribute.

Check your example for distractors.

Present the example.

Label the critical attributes or elements in the example.

Present exceptions.

Let's now take a look at each of these principles in greater depth.

Identify the Critical Attributes(s) of the Present Learning

In trying to determine the critical attribute, ask yourself which attribute is invariant whenever the concept is encountered. For example, in foreign languages, one critical attribute of modifiers is that they agree in number with the nouns they modify.

Select from Students' Own Lives Some Previous Knowledge or Experience That Exemplifies the Same Critical Attribute

Think about how you can harness students' past knowledge to accelerate learning. For example, students' familiarity with the modifiers *this* and *that* can be brought forward to accelerate learning of agreement between nouns and modifiers and increase the probability of correspondence between singular and plural nouns and adjectives in the future. Examples might include *this book, these books, that boy,* and *those boys.* It is critical that the teacher select the example, so it contains the same attribute, is valid, and has no confusing or irrelevant elements.

Seldom can such examples be generated on the spot; they take a good degree of thought and testing. Consequently, at initial presentation we should not ask students to supply examples. If we do, we are taking the chance of introducing confusion or irrelevancies at the beginning of learning, which is prime time for learning and remembering both errors and correct responses.

Check Your Example for Distractors

In an attempt to make learning interesting, it is possible to introduce distractors; however, teachers should remember the following admonition: Don't bring an elephant into the classroom to teach the concept gray. Notice your own reaction to the following examples: *this terrorist, those terrorists* versus *this book, those books.*

Students' attention can easily be diverted from the critical attribute being identified, and the students may become focused on feelings elicited by the example. At times, we may wish to imbue learning with emotional overtones; however, most of the time, emotions (with the exception of interest) can direct students' attention away from the critical attribute the example was designed to teach.

To teach a political concept by introducing it through a current controversial situation could stir up those in favor and those against. These emotions will most certainly distract from the concept being taught. For example, introducing the notion of legalized marijuana or legalized prostitution could shift a student's attention away from learning the discriminators that separate legal from illegal actions. It is better to use examples such as lobbying or cold medicines, which do not have such emotional overtones.

Present the Example

The teacher presents a well-thought-out example in simple and unambiguous language: "Think of the way you use *this* and *these* to modify singular and plural nouns: *this book* and *these books.* You use *that* for the singular *that boy* and the modifier *those* for the plural *those boys.* In English, we don't do that with all modifiers, but in foreign languages adjectives are made singular or plural to match the nouns they modify. In Spanish, the singular *casa blanca* becomes *casas blancas* when plural."

Label the Critical Attributes or Elements in the Example

Make sure that your students have successfully perceived the discriminators you're teaching, rather than having focused their attention on some irrelevant element.

To continue with our foreign language example, you might say, "Notice that *casa*, meaning 'house,' is singular, so *blanca* is singular. The word *casas*, meaning 'houses,' is plural, so the modifier *blancas* also must be plural. In the same way we say, 'sombrero rojo' and 'sombreros rojos.'"

Present Exceptions

Finally, after students have a well-developed understanding of the concept, if there are exceptions, present them, so students know the limits of the generalization they have learned. For example, in English, *hair* is a singular noun, but in Italian it is plural, so it needs a plural modifier.

In this book, we are attempting to use examples that will hook into your own past teaching experience, so you will bring additional meaning to the generalizations we present. This should enable you to learn pedagogical principles faster, remember them longer, and transfer them more readily into your future teaching.

Our identifying, labeling, and demonstrating basic principles of learning should hook into your past teaching experiences. You bring that knowledge forward to accelerate achievement of increased teaching effectiveness.

> *"The brain is a pattern recognition device. Experience builds those patterns."*

2. Provide Experience

Meaning isn't inherent in material but in the relation of the material to the learner's past experience. In many cases, students have little or no experience in the content we are teaching.

The brain is a pattern recognition device. Experience builds those patterns. From those patterns emerge concepts (a group of perceptively dissimilar things that have similar attributes, such as mammal, fraction, conflict, and door) that the brain recognizes. From the experiences that build the patterns and subsequent concepts, we apply language and give names to the concepts. We are then able to apply those labels and concepts to new situations.

When a young child sees a cat and learns that it is called a kitty, for example, the child erroneously begins to refer to anything furry as "kitty." In time, multiple experiences refine the concept of cat for the child so that cat is perceived as different from tiger and skunk (yet the child identifies a tremendous variety of sizes, shapes, and colors of cat correctly as cats). By learning the attributes of cats, the child would later be able to identify an animal he or she has never seen before as a cat (application).

Build the Concept

In school, we often try to teach a concept and its name without taking into consideration the experience necessary to build the pattern in the brain (such as memorizing definitions or formulas). We then find ourselves confounded when students have trouble applying the concept to new situations. When students cannot apply learning to a new situation, it is because they do not really "have" the concept.

Concept building comes from experience with many different examples of the concept. When students do not have the experiences necessary to get the concept we are attempting to teach, we can provide it for them. This is the way we develop number sense in children: by providing lots of experience with numbers. Likewise, problem-solving skills are learned best when we give students multiple experiences with real problems to solve (as opposed to applying an algorithm repeatedly to different sets of numbers or a page of similar word problems at the end of the chapter).

Students who come to us from homes where parents began to read to them at an early age have an experience that has built important language concepts, and we add to this experience. Students who haven't come from this type of background need us to provide these experiences to build the basic language concepts necessary to support new learning. Assessment provides us with this essential information, so we can plan instructional experiences and determine whether students have the prerequisite knowledge to support the new learning.

Take a Trip

Field trips can be powerful in providing the experience necessary for students to understand curriculum. In the early grades, for example, we teach the concepts of community, producers, consumers, and service providers. Field trips to food distribution centers, bakeries, markets, and police and fire departments can be powerful in building concepts on which we build language and understanding. I know a teacher who, when teaching ancient civilization and how archeologists study it (something very few sixth graders have any experience with), creates an archeological dig. In this dig she buries several novel artifacts at a variety of depths. The students must then measure, create a grid, map, and explore the dig, recording all of their findings and the specific location and depth where they were found. From this they extrapolate age, function, and relationships, much as a real archeologist would, thus making the learning much more meaningful to the students.

3. Provide a Function

A third way to make material meaningful is to provide a function for the material, a reason for learning it. The human brain learns almost effortlessly when there is a sensible reason to learn. You see this as you pursue a hobby, where you learn a tremendous amount without any effort at all. This is because learning related to your hobby makes sense to you. By providing a real reason to learn something, you dramatically improve the ease of learning it.

Many of us took cooking classes in school, but most of us really didn't learn to cook until we had to start feeding ourselves or our family. This is another example of task authenticity, doing something for a real reason. In the following examples in Box 8.1, the learning has been given a function, so there is an enhanced purpose for learning it.

Box 8.1   Authentic Tasks for Authentic Learning

The following are some examples of learning embedded in an authentic context:

· learning scale in designing a school garden
· learning linear measurement by building a drying rack
· learning short *A* words to make a short *A* book to be shared with peers
· learning to write a business letter to canvas companies for donations to a class project
· learning to read directions carefully to build a wheelbarrow
· learning to calculate percentages by having to add tax to the items your class is selling for the winter holiday boutique
· learning word processing skills to create bibliographies for class reports
· learning engineering skills to construct floats for the Rose Parade

---

4. Use Mnemonics

Sometimes it is not possible to identify in our students a past experience that might facilitate current learning. For example, it is difficult to make classification systems, tables, and lists meaningful, so they can be learned and remembered easily. Consequently, we need to invent artificial meaning to associate with the material. "Every good boy does fine" helps us remember the musical notes *e, g, b, d, f.* We call this artificial meaning a mnemonic device. Here are some examples of mnemonic devices:

"It ads" stands for iamb, troque, anapest, dactyl, and spandi (in poetic feet).

"Dessert makes you bigger in the middle." The word dessert is bigger in the middle than the word desert. It has more s's than desert.

A principal should be your "pal," so the word ends that way.

Thirty days hath September, April, June, and November. All the rest have 31, except February.

Yours is not to reason why, just invert and multiply.

Latitude is like lateral (or sideways), horizontal rings around the earth. There's an *at* in latitude, like your belt is *at* your middle.

Longitude has the word *long* in it, and goes from the top to bottom of the earth. It has a *g* in it, which has a tail below the line and points to the bottom of a map, and a *t* in it, which points to the top, so you can remember longitude goes from the top, or North Pole, to the bottom, or South Pole.

When your students experience difficulty remembering something and you can't build in enough meaning, encourage them to create their own mnemonic or develop several mnemonics so each student can choose the one that is most vivid and meaningful.

Obviously, when we can introduce real meaning in a concept, we should not distract the student with the creation of mnemonic devices. When real meaning is unavailable, however, mnemonics can assist learning.

MAKING SURE TO MAKE IT REAL

In summary, when we can relate material to our learners' past experience, we make that material much more meaningful and hence more quickly learned. When students do not have the experiences necessary for the material to be meaningful, we should provide experiences both within and outside of the school, if possible. Providing a real function for the material to be learned also builds rationale and meaning for the student.

When it is not possible to use experience to assist in learning and remembering lists, classification systems, or labels, we can create artificial meaning by using a mnemonic device.

Making material meaningful returns large dividends not only in students' accelerated learning but also in their retention of the material. These two learning dividends are, again, limited only by your ingenuity and creativity as you make your own material meaningful to students.

Chapter 9

Checking Your Students' Understanding

Guide for Group Discussion or Individual Study

Objectives: *Participants will:*
a. Identify techniques for checking their students' understanding while teaching.
b. Generate techniques that can be used in subsequent class sessions.
c. Try out techniques to determine which contribute most to teachers' diagnostic information and students' understanding.

Anticipatory Set: List some techniques you use to check your students' understanding while you are teaching.

Input & Modeling: Read the chapter "Checking Your Students' Understanding."

Checking for Understanding & Guided Practice: Identify four techniques that check students' understanding without the necessity of correcting tests or papers.

Check your original list to see if you have been using all four techniques. Develop examples of any omitted techniques that you could use in subsequent classes. Exchange techniques with other participants.

Independent Practice: Experiment with techniques for checking your students' understanding in subsequent classes and determine which are most effective.

Chapter **9**

Checking Your Students' Understanding

To say that you have taught when students haven't learned is to say you have sold when no one has bought. But how can you know that students have learned without spending hours correcting tests and papers?

CHECKING FOR UNDERSTANDING DURING TEACHING

We believe the job of the teacher is to inspire, not perspire. In this chapter, you'll learn four ways to check students' understanding while you are teaching (not at ten o'clock at night when you're correcting papers). As a result, you won't continue to teach unlearned material that can accumulate like a snowball and eventually engulf the student in confusion and despair. Likewise, you can avoid spending additional, precious class time on a skill the students have acquired and can move on to other learning.

FOUR COMMON ERRORS THAT TEACHERS MAKE

In attempting to check for understanding during a lesson, teachers may commit four common errors.

Excessive Use of "OK?"

The most common error is a teacher's ubiquitous "OK?," with the assumption that student silence means everything is OK and they understand. For example, "We've finished this chapter, OK?" or "Let's move on to the next section, OK?" Which student is going to be brave—or brash—enough to say, "No, it's not OK. You're going too fast!"?

Asking Questions That Assume Your Students Understand

A common way to check students' understanding is by asking, "You all understand, don't you?" or "You don't have any questions, do you?" Few students are willing to admit publicly that they don't understand. In fact, most students work hard to keep their teacher from discovering that they don't know or can't do something. Don't give your students the opportunity to fool you by asking ineffective questions. One of the most important pieces of information teachers can have is the knowledge that students have not yet acquired necessary understanding.

Asking Students If They Have Any Questions

Another frequently used but not very useful method for checking students' understanding is the query "Now, does anyone have a question?" Too often such a question carries the implication that if students do have questions they obviously weren't listening or are not very bright. This kind of question can also be an invitation for students to divert teachers by asking for unneeded information (e.g., "Do we have to type it?"). Sometimes students think the teacher wants questions, and, even though no information is needed, they try to oblige. Students also may be employing a delay tactic to avoid getting to work or moving on to new content.

Questioning Your Students' Understanding
When You Know They Have Not Been Listening

Sometimes teachers use checking for understanding as a disciplinary tool. For example, the teacher notices Mary's attention is wandering and calls on her to answer a question when Mary obviously has not heard the information and, even worse, may not have heard the question. Directing the question at Mary will refocus her attention, but it also strips her of her dignity, as she has been caught publicly being wrong (she hasn't even heard the question!). This is the last thing we want to do with a student. In addition to creating unpleasant feeling tone in the room, stripping students of dignity causes their cognitive functions related to learning to shut down (the reptilian part of the brain takes over and they go into survival mode). This is exactly what we do not want to occur. There are many more effective and productive techniques for reengaging a student's wandering attention.

All four of these dysfunctional methods for checking students' understanding can result in a teacher's proceeding to the next topic, blissfully unaware that students are lost. This problem can be prevented (and hours of correction of papers saved) by employing any one, or a combination, of the following techniques. Remember, the purpose of checking for understanding is to obtain evidence of how much learning has taken place, so we can adjust our teaching appropriately. Also, as an overlay to all of these techniques, we want to keep in mind the research on wait time. Under most conditions, when you ask a question or pose a problem, you should provide time for the students to think. When we provide wait time two things happen:

> The number of students who think of the answer increases (ideally we want all students thinking of all the answers).

> The quality of the answers they think of (assuming that it involves more than the recall of a fact) increases.

We also want to be sure not to name a student to answer before asking the question. Instead, beam the question to the whole group. Then, no one knows who will have to answer and all will begin to think (raising level of concern).

FOUR EFFECTIVE TECHNIQUES FOR CHECKING YOUR STUDENTS' UNDERSTANDING IN CLASS

1. Signaled Answers

A simple way to check understanding is to pose a question, or a problem and have every student signal the answer (see Box 9.1).

The variety is endless but the effect is the same: evidence of understanding or the lack thereof. Our goal is to have all students thinking and engaged in the learning.

Keep an Eye on Your Students

If students are using their peripheral vision to check other students' answers, two very positive things are actually occurring: The student who doesn't know or is unsure is using an excellent learning strategy—looking around to find out—and the teacher sees which students are looking around or not signaling. This is just the type of information the teacher needs (i.e., who doesn't have it yet). Are there many students looking

Box 9.1 Getting Students to Signal Answers

The following are some examples of how to elicit signaled answers from students:

"Look at the first multiple choice question. Decide which answer you would select. When I say, 'show me,' hold up that number of fingers."

"Which operation would I use to solve this problem?" (Note: After asking the initial question, pause. The length of the pause or wait time should be adjusted based on the complexity of the learning or on the needs of the students in this case, and in the following cases.)

"Show me if it is addition, subtraction, multiplication, or division." (pause)

"How many times will the divisor go into the dividend?" (pause) "Show me."

"To the right of what number will the decimal go?" (pause) "Show me the number using your fingers."

"Show me, with your arm, which way the barometer would go if a storm were coming."

"Show a *D* for dependent clause and an *I* for an independent clause."

"Is this a long *a* or a short *a* sound?"

"I will state a series of conclusions. Show me if they are *V*, valid, or *I*, invalid."

around, only a few, or none at all? It is this evidence that the teacher uses to adjust instruction.

Explain Yourself

Occasionally, some teachers think that older students will feel silly, embarrassed, or resent this type of classroom probing of their understanding. It has been the experience of teachers and university professors that students respond enthusiastically when they employ these techniques.

This is, of course, after it has been explained to them that we do not want to proceed with instruction if they don't understand the material (only to be revealed on a graded exam), nor do we want to bore them with material they already know. When signaled answers are accompanied by an explanation of the reason why a certain response is correct, students can, without penalty, correct misunderstandings and learn to apply the generalization to new questions or situations.

Have Students Use Hand Signals

Students can use a great variety of signals to indicate answers. The most effective signals are those that visually represent the answer. For example, if you were checking students' understanding of how to punctuate sentences, students might be taught to use the following: To show a comma, they could use a curved index finger; a period could be a point of the finger, an exclamation point could be a vertical finger (be sure to specify which finger!), and a question mark could be a curved hand on top of the straight fingers of the other hand.

Numbers are easy to show, as are members of numbered categories (e.g., mammals = 1, birds = 2). Different types of angles can be demonstrated using an arm (e.g., bent arm = acute, straight arm = obtuse). Light wave amplitude for various colors may be shown by hand motions of shallow, short waves or deeper, longer waves. The only limit to types of signals is your imagination.

"The job of the teacher is to inspire, not perspire."

Students who are not used to signaling their answers may require some time to be taught the signal system and to understand that all students—not simply the students who usually volunteer—will be expected to use it. Many times you will want to tell the students to think of their answer but not show it until told to; this way, everyone has a chance to think and not just mimic the first to respond in the group.

The signal system does not give concrete evidence that all students understand the skill or concept you are teaching. It does, however, provide a very good indicator of most of the students' understanding. It is quick, involves all of the students, and can be immediately read by the teacher, so adjustments in instruction can be made immediately.

2. Choral Responses

A second method of checking students' understanding is to ask the group a question and get a choral response (e.g., "Is this an example of dactylic or iambic?"). The strength as well as the correctness of the response can give valuable clues as to whether most students know the answer.

Precautions

Be aware that choral responses have two problems. One is that some students don't answer. As a result, the teacher doesn't know if those students know the answer but are covert learners (i.e., respond within themselves but not aloud) or whether they don't know the answer. The second problem with choral responses is that some of the students who do respond may be coat tailing (i.e., moving their mouths without actually saying words, just as many of us do in the second chorus of the national anthem because we don't know all the words). Teaching dividends from choral responses are greater than testing dividends.

Benefits

In spite of these two problems, choral responses have value. The strength of the response alerts the teacher to the probable level of student understanding. A weak response indicates that more instruction may be needed. A strong response indicates readiness to move on. Choral responses are also an excellent way for a student who doesn't know the answer to learn the correct response without visibility or humiliation.

Choral responses also allow the students who have gone to the effort of thinking of the answer a chance to express it, which can be more gratifying to the student than not having that chance. This is especially true of younger students who are extremely eager to participate all of the time. Choral responses also can be used to inject novelty into the lesson by changing the participation mode. It is also a good technique to use at the beginning stages of learning because it allows students who are comfortable with the content to respond, and it allows those who are unsure to sit back and hear a correct response. Does this technique give you evidence that reliably indicates student learning? No, but it can give the teacher a good indication of the level of understanding of the class or group by the strength and accuracy of the response.

3. Sample Individual Response

A third technique for checking understanding is for the teacher to beam a question to the whole class (e.g., "Be ready to give me an example of this generalization.") and then call on individual students. The teacher can then make an inference on the basis of the stratum of the class each student represents: If a bright student is confused, a justifiable inference is that most of the students don't understand. If an average student doesn't know, the inference is that a substantial portion of the class needs to spend more time on the subject. If a slower student responds correctly, the class probably is ready to move on.

The question arises of what to do when only a few students remain confused. If this occurs early in the teaching of new content, it is justifiable to spend more time on that content. The result may be overlearning by the rest of the students, but as long as examples are new rather than repetitious, which would create boredom, retention of the material will be increased for all students.

If considerable time has been spent on the content and there still remains a small group that hasn't achieved the learning, it is better to plan an opportunity to reteach those students while the rest of the class is engaged in another activity. The teacher can heterogeneously group the students with a peer tutor (if this is viable for the content) or plan a time to meet with those students while the rest of the class is engaged in practice or extension activities. What is most important is for the teacher to recognize when some students do not understand the content and then to do something about it. This is even more critical when the content follows a dependent sequence (i.e., when subsequent learning is based on the successful acquisition of previous learning). Moving on with unlearned material creates a negative prognosis for future understanding.

4. Individual Private Response

A fourth method of checking for understanding is to pose a question or problem and have the students write a brief response. While they are writing, the teacher can circulate among the students to assess the accuracy of their responses.

By giving more than one question or problem, the teacher can assess quite thoroughly the level of understanding of the entire class. The teacher can also select particularly vivid or illuminating student responses to be presented to the total class, which adds variety and increases everyone's understanding of the concept, generalization, or discrimination being presented.

What evidence of learning does this technique give the teacher? It provides thorough and accurate information from all of the students during the lesson, instead of later from class assignments or tests. The disadvantage is that it takes some time, though not a lot, to monitor students' responses. However, this time is worthwhile because teachers can see immediately whether the concepts and skills are accurately understood and catch and correct errors or misconceptions before they are practiced.

None of these methods are intended as a thorough assessment of student performance. Rather, they are intended to gauge student understanding throughout the instructional process for on-the-spot adjustments that make learning more accurate and predictable. Examination of student work is the most reliable indicator of what the students have been able to internalize and apply and, as a result, is essential to planning further instruction.

ASSESSING UNDERSTANDING USING TESTS, PAPERS, OR OBSERVATIONS OF PERFORMANCE

Eventually, students must demonstrate achievement of learning by producing a product. Usually this is a test, paper, or performance.

Tests

In written exams, teachers need to be aware of students who have a facility for running off at the pen and sounding brilliant, even though they may not understand a concept. Unless a ponderous research paper is the objective, it is wise to limit the amount of writing permitted. A one-sentence, one-paragraph, or one-page answer requires a clear understanding and prohibits fuzzy rambling. Size limitations also give the teacher less to correct and leave no question as to the student's comprehension. Limitations also set a premium on quality rather than quantity, a highly desirable intellectual goal.

Papers

Short papers (one to five pages) allow teachers to grade quickly and return papers promptly, giving students immediate feedback as to what they have achieved and what they still need to learn. Teacher comments written on those papers are essential if students are to have specific knowledge of what they know and what they need to learn. Grades simply tell a student the paper was acceptable or unacceptable but not why, and they do not tell what needs to be added or changed.

Performance

Some learning can be measured only by direct observation of performance (e.g., athletics, music, arts, teaching); that performance becomes the test to be evaluated. The criteria for a performance need to be made explicit, so feedback can be specific.

Combined Assessments

In summary, we suggest that you employ a combination of techniques, making sure to check your students' understanding throughout the instructional process by eliciting signals, choral responses, sampled individual responses, and individual written responses. Eventually, tests, papers, projects, or a demonstration of the target learning is necessary to determine how well students understand the concepts and generalizations—and their relationships—and use their creative-thinking and problem-solving skills.

You will be amazed by how such dipsticking while you are teaching contributes to your knowledge of what has been learned and what needs to be retaught, and subsequent tests, papers, and performances will reflect an increase in student achievement.

Chapter 10

Practice Doesn't Make Perfect:
Designing Effective Practice

Guide for Group Discussion or Individual Study

Objectives: *Participants will:*
a. State and answer the four questions related to practice.
b. Design teaching plans that incorporate principles of practice in subsequent classes.

Anticipatory Set: List some factors that you think should be incorporated in students' practice to produce the most improvement in cognitive, affective, or psychomotor performance.

Input & Modeling: Read the chapter "Practice Doesn't Make Perfect."

Checking for Understanding & Guided Practice: List and answer the four questions about practice you stated earlier. Classify your original list in terms of the four answers.

Identify learnings that have been difficult for your students and then design ways of incorporating the four principles of practice in your class sessions.

Discuss the conditions under which class time should be used for practice and those conditions when practice should be done outside of class.

Independent Practice: Try these teaching techniques in subsequent classes and determine which are most effective.

Chapter 10

Practice Doesn't Make Perfect

Designing Effective Practice

Practice, "doing it again," does not make perfect. Witness the freeway drivers who "do it again" every day but don't improve. You surely know someone to whose house you dread going for dinner. That person may have been practicing cooking for years but still can't master it.

If one automatically improved with practice, all older teachers would be better than younger ones, and we know that is not the case.

MASTERY ONLY BEGINS WITH AUTOMATICITY

In Chapter 8, we learned that the more meaningful we can make what we teach, the quicker it will be learned. In fact, meaning is the most powerful determinate of time necessary for learning. There are many things that must be learned by students that, in and of themselves, have very little meaning. Math facts, vowel sounds, some math processes, spelling words, and sight vocabulary, for example, can't be made so meaningful that they require only one-shot learning. These skills must be practiced until students internalize them and reach a level of automaticity in their use.

Automaticity is essential so that learners can use their cognitive energy in solving the problems, deriving text meaning, and using written communication that require these skills as tools. We can see when this hasn't occurred, for example, as students who haven't mastered multiplication facts struggle with division or as those who are focused on decoding every word in a text lack comprehension.

Other types of learnings, such as the content of social studies chapters and science knowledge, concepts, and generalizations, contain so much material that one does need to study to internalize it.

PRACTICING PROPERLY: FOUR PRINCIPLES TO IMPROVE PERFORMANCE

For practice to improve performance, whether it be in basketball, physics, writing, math, vocational education, or teaching, that practice must be designed and conducted according to four psychological principles. These principles constitute the answers to four questions you must ask when you design practice for your students.

In this chapter, you will learn to ask and answer those four critical questions so students' practice increases their learning and improves their performance, rather than just taking up time.

Question 1: **How much material should be practiced at one time?**

Answer: **A short meaningful amount. Always use meaning (not mathematics!) to divide your content.**

The brain's working memory only holds five to seven chunks of information. A chunk is a meaningful unit. For example, a chunk can be a word, a concept, a generalization, or a series of generalizations. For learnings that are discrete bits, such as math facts or spelling words, and have no real relation to each other, a chunk is one, such as one math fact or one spelling word. For learnings that are more comprehensive but related, such as a stanza of a poem or the effects of the war on the economy, the size of the chunk is much larger. When you are designing practice for discrete bits of information, you'll have very few bits to be practiced at one time. Studying the entire 7 times tables is too much and will overload working memory. Studying three to four of the facts in the 7 times tables is much more effective.

When practicing social studies content, for example, you'll have the same few chunks, but the chunks will contain more information. Have your students learn the content in meaningful chunks, as in the following:

political relations of the countries before the war

the event that sparked the war

events of the war

the aftermath of the war

By designing instruction in this way, there is no question that your students' learning yields will increase.

When teaching, introduce a short meaningful chunk to your students. Then give several examples or go over it again in a different way. Make sure you check their understanding and their reasonable accomplishment before you move on (see Chapter 9, "Checking Your Students' Understanding"). Then, you can introduce another chunk to the students or have them practice the first chunk you introduced (see Box 10.1).

Box 10.1   Examples for Chunking Practice

Practice working on writing topic sentences. After the initial lessons, give the students several paragraphs with no topic sentences and have them write two possible topic sentences for each paragraph.

Practice learning three or four vocabulary words until they are clearly known, then add three or four more (the same applies with spelling words or math facts).

Practice the identification of dependent and independent clauses. When most of the students have achieved understanding, practice the use of the comma in sentences that begin with dependent clauses.

Practice the use of the apostrophe in contractions. After that has been learned, practice the use of the apostrophe in possessives.

Practice learning the critical attributes of algae. After they have been learned, move on to fungi.

Practice identification of the setting of a story. After that has been reasonably accomplished, move on to plot.

Practice with regular verbs. After they are learned, move to irregular verbs.

Practice only one part of a performance. When that part has been reasonably (not perfectly) learned, move on to the next part. While you may introduce the total performance to show where the part to be practiced belongs, students' practice should be focused on a short, meaningful part.

Practicing in this way is an effective method of getting the material internalized because it allows working memory to process the material with enough frequency to build neural pathways into long-term memory, which is why we practice. Too much material at one time overloads working memory, preventing it from moving the material into long-term memory.

Question 2: **How long should a practice period last?**

Answer: **Practice should last a short time, so the students exert intense effort and have the intent to learn.**

The key words in the answer to this question are *intent* to learn and *intense,* or highly motivated, effort on the part of the student. Consequently, because human beings do not easily sustain focus and intensity for long periods, the practice period on any one aspect of learning should be short. Several short, highly motivated practice periods yield more improvement than a long one, which often deteriorates into lessening of effort and increased distraction.

You can literally hear this happen in a classroom. When a practice assignment is initially given, the room is generally very quiet and focused. After about ten minutes, you begin to hear voices and other noises, indicating that students are getting off task. You can also see it in their work. More mistakes tend to get made in the last half of the assignment, where student intent and focus have waned.

Unfortunately, much practice is done with the motivation to get it over with, rather than to get it learned. We, as teachers, contribute to this when we acknowledge or reward finishing, rather than learning or quality performance. Instead of asking, "Have you finished it?" we should ask, "Have you learned it?"

When asking groups of practicing educators how many of a certain type of math problem or sentence punctuation exercise a student would need to do to learn the skill, the answer is usually five to ten problems. Frequently, though, the assignment given is twenty to twenty-five problems in length. This, too, creates the get-it-done mentality, rather than an intent-to-learn motive. Obviously, the

> *"Instead of asking, 'Have you finished it?' we should ask, 'Have you learned it?'"*

more complex the task, the more time needed to practice. Even then, short, intense practice periods yield the greatest learning dividends.

Often, a practice period may be broken into segments, with students practicing different things rather than practicing one thing for the total period (see Box 10.2).

Short, intense practice periods are equally important for psychomotor skills, a fact known for some time by music, dance, and drama teachers and athletic coaches. In fact, you will usually see practice in these areas designed congruently with how the human best learns. When practicing a musical piece or basketball, the students do not practice the entire piece or game. They practice small, meaningful amounts (e.g., the first twelve bars or a post pattern). They practice for a short period (five to ten minutes) and then switch to something else (scales, free throws, etc.) for another brief period. This keeps the students alert and focused, while maintaining their

---

Box 10.2   Keep Practice Short and Segmented

Instruct students in the following ways:

"Practice six math problems of the type we are working on. Then, for five minutes, practice a math fact family for speed. Then, do six more of the math problems."

"Work on your phonics word family for five to ten minutes, then work with sight-word flash cards with a neighbor. When you've got them, reread the pages in the story we just read." (For young children, maximizing reading of familiar text is effective in internalizing decoding skills and sight vocabulary.)

"Outline the organization of your composition and then write a rough draft of your introductory paragraph. Have a peer read it and give you feedback (assuming you have taught the students to do this). Then, begin the body of the composition."

Spend ten minutes practicing dependent clauses, followed by ten minutes practicing possessives. Go back to check dependent clauses, then move on to descriptive words. Go back to check apostrophes with descriptive phrases. Finally, put them all together: "Although the insufferable man's language offended us, we managed to sustain our equanimity."

Practice the critical attributes of algae. When they are reasonably learned, move on to fungi. After that is learned, check that the attributes of algae are retained and move on to liverworts. Spend a short, intense period on each and check back, so students know they are accountable not only for learning but also for remembering what was learned.

---

intent to learn. Only when they have reasonably achieved each component do they incorporate it into bigger pieces and, eventually, the entire performance.

Question 3: **How often should students practice?**

Answer: **For new learning, mass practice; for older learning, distribute practice.**

There are two answers to this question, depending on whether the learning is new to the student. New learning is not very durable, so several practice periods scheduled close together will yield very rapid learning. Practice periods that are close together in time are called massed practice. Massed practice is accomplished when you employ several different examples embodying the same principle, several questions requiring the same discrimination, several problems involving the same operation, or several different situations requiring the same mode of attack. This type of closely spaced practice is necessary to create the neural pathways or connections needed for easy retrieval of the material or performance of the task. Students use this principle when they cram for an exam. Material can be quickly learned, but it also can be quickly forgotten unless the practice schedule changes.

Once something is understood or has been learned, the practice periods need to be spaced farther apart. Increasing time intervals between practice sessions is called distributed practice, and it yields long remembering. We distribute practice when we periodically review previously learned material.

For the most effective use of practice time, practice should be massed at the beginning of learning. Then, practice periods should be changed to a distributed schedule. Translated into your class periods, this means you should go over something several times when you first introduce it. If you move on to something else, come back to the new material again and review it at the end of the period. At the next class period, check to make sure the material is remembered. If it is, you don't need to review it until a few class periods later. If the material is forgotten, you will need to reteach it and review it again the next time the class meets.

Homework can be an excellent opportunity to mass practice a new concept or skill (providing it was learned and mistakes won't be practiced). Homework also can be used to distribute practice on previously learned material.

> "Most of us have had the experience of monitoring our students taking a state achievement test and, to our horror, seeing them miss problems that we killed ourselves teaching earlier in the year. This is often because, when teaching the skills, we massed their practice and then moved on to new material. If we do not distribute practice on previously learned material, one can reliably predict that it will fall from memory."

Addressing the Standards

With the current emphasis on state achievement tests, most of us have had the experience of monitoring our students taking a standardized exam and, to our horror, seeing them miss problems that we killed ourselves teaching earlier in the year. This is often because, when teaching the skills, we massed their practice and then moved on to new material. If we do not distribute practice on previously learned material, one can reliably predict that it will fall from memory.

Another factor in students' propensity to forget is the depth of initial learning. Material learned at a very shallow level disappears much more quickly than material that is well understood. For material to be learned in a way that is not forgotten and is readily applied, it needs to be taught in depth. Covering a lot of material with no in-depth instruction virtually guarantees quick forgetting.

Upon examination of state curriculum standards, one can see that there isn't enough time in each year to accomplish all of them. This abundance of curriculum at each grade level is compounded by the same characteristics in textbooks, which need to be saleable in the major markets and, therefore, encompass each state's curriculum standards. State standards and textbooks create a tremendous pressure on teachers to cover the material. To combat this coverage mentality, many districts are identifying curriculum standards that have greater priority and focusing instruction on teaching them in depth. These prioritized standards are the concepts and skills that have the greatest applicability to other situations in life.

While a massed and then a distributed practice schedule may seem to consume a great deal of time when you could be moving on to new learning, you will find that time is saved in the long run because students remember better and can use what they have learned. Explaining why you are scheduling practice in this way helps your students schedule their own practice and review periods, so they not only learn faster but also remember longer.

Question 4: How will students know how well they have done?

Answer: Give specific knowledge of results.

To practice without letting students know how they are doing (i.e., giving knowledge of results) is usually a waste of time. At first, the answer to the question "How am I doing?" needs to come from the teacher, who sets the criteria for excellence in performance. Once students know the criteria for excellence, they can evaluate their own performance or use materials to check correctness.

Students receive knowledge of results as the teacher asks questions, has students signal responses, or instructs them to write brief responses on paper. After hearing student answers or viewing student work, the teacher tells students the correct answer and the reason why it is correct. By doing this, students learn the criteria to be used later in evaluating their own responses.

Let's practice what we preach and mass your practice on the information in this chapter.

Ideas in Action: Mass Practice Now

On a sheet of paper, write the four questions to be asked in designing students' practice.

In a short phrase, write the answer to each question and an example of what that might look like with a skill you teach in your classroom.

Check your answers by reviewing the information on the previous pages.

Distribute your practice by later checking your recall of the questions and answers.

Most important, practice implementing these four principles of effective practice as you conduct or assign practice in your classes. Your students' accelerated learning and increased retention will be ample evidence of the success of your efforts.

DESIGNING VALUABLE PRACTICE IS KEY

This chapter focused on four psychological principles that we can use to design practice sessions, so they effectively help students internalize the skills, concepts, and generalizations of the curriculum. Another aspect to consider is the quality of the tasks we have the students actually practice. This is why it is so important to be very clear as to what our objective is. In other words, what exactly do we want the students to be able to do as a result of this instruction?

Know Your Objective

The practice activity should match the objective. In selecting activities for practice, it is important to analyze them for this congruence. Do the activities have the student practicing the same skill that has been taught, or is it a related skill?

If our objective is for the student to read a selected piece of literature and identify the main idea, then that is what the practice activity should be: reading pieces and identifying their main idea. A related, but not relevant, activity would be selecting the best main idea from several possible main ideas. The first activity involves reading and generating the main idea; the second involves selecting a main idea from a menu. These are different cognitive skills. If our objective is to have the students read and summarize material, then the practice should be to have students reading and identifying the main ideas or events necessary to the plot.

This is what a summary is. What would not be relevant would be to have the students fill in a story frame with events from the story as they occurred. This activity has students sequencing, not identifying what is important or essential.

Quality Activities Equal Quality Learning

When selecting practice activities, it is imperative that we ask ourselves, "Does this activity practice the same cognitive skill we are working on?" Many activities we typically associate with a skill do not, upon closer examination, in fact practice that skill. Another area to consider when designing practice is how much thinking is required of the student. Many readily available activities require the student to do very little. Be it bubbling a correct choice, filling in a word blank, or matching a word with its correct definition, the demands on the learner to use literacy skills may be quite low.

We want students using language, generating thought, and fully maximizing their use of reading skills. Rather than matching words with their definition, have the students write their vocabulary in meaning-loaded sentences (sentences that demonstrate that the student knows the meaning of the word). Rather than having students fill in blanks in a paragraph to show they can create meaningful text, have them summarize their knowledge about the same topic to demonstrate their thinking in depth. Many of our students come from language-deprived backgrounds. Having them engaged in activities that require a greater use of language and thought is the productive road toward overcoming that deficit.

Chapter 11

Guiding Your Students' Initial Practice

Guide for Group Discussion or Individual Study

Objective:

Participants will:
a. Tell why it is important to be available to guide initial practice with new learning.
b. Generate examples of upcoming lessons and how they might structure guided practice for those lessons.

Anticipatory Set:

What are some problems that arise when you turn new learning over to the students to practice for the first time?

Input and Modeling:

Read the chapter "Guiding Your Students' Initial Practice."

Checking for Understanding & Guided Practice:

Have the participants discuss why initial support for new learning is essential for efficient learning.

Have the participants generate and share examples of lesson objectives and how they might guide the students' initial attempts at practicing the new learning.

Independent Practice:

Purposefully design guided practice for your lessons when it is needed.

Chapter 11

Guiding Your Students' Initial Practice

Ⅰt is very tempting to assume that if the teacher has provided an excellent explanation or demonstration of new learning, then students should be able to accomplish a similar task independently using that learning. Unfortunately, even when students are focused and motivated, they frequently need more support and guidance before being given assignments to complete independently (e.g., seatwork or homework). An underlying premise for planning effective lessons is called degree of guidance.

DETERMINING THE DEGREE OF GUIDANCE

When beginning to plan for effective instruction, teachers should select the content standard, establish the objective (based on assessment of student knowledge in that standard), and choose the final student performance (product or test) that will validate the acquisition of that learning.

Initially, teachers provide a maximum degree of guidance with new material through input and modeling of those skills, concepts, or generalizations. After the teacher sees—through checking for understanding—that the students are grasping the new information, the teacher can begin to reduce the degree of guidance. As guidance is reduced, the students take more responsibility for using the material and engaging in guided practice.

The type of guidance must be appropriate for the type of learning. Guided practice for memorizing factual information—such as math facts, vocabulary words, or people, places, and events—will look quite different from learning how to test a hypothesis with scientific inquiry or develop a cooperative research project. Guided practice for mathematical problem-solving experiences requires the teacher to monitor students' discussions and probe their thought process.

TEACHING KNOWLEDGEABLY

It is here that we reach a critical point in learning. New learning is like wet cement: It can easily be damaged. Mistakes that are practiced at the beginning of learning have long-lasting consequences that are hard to eradicate. Consequently, when turning material over to the students, it is essential that the initial attempt to use that material be guided by an expert. This expert is usually the teacher, but other adults or peers could be trained in the skills of coaching during guided practice.

An effective instructor minimizes the chances for error and provides the feedback essential to improve performance. If students are performing outside their competence level, they are going to make errors. This is a normal part of the learning process. What happens after students have made those errors is critical for efficient learning. Are the errors identified? Is information given that allows students to improve their performance? Or are the errors practiced repeatedly?

Practice does not make perfect—it makes permanent. If you pick up a tennis racquet and play for a while holding the racquet incorrectly, it is much more difficult (and takes far more time) to relearn to hold it correctly. This is why people involved in physical performances (visual art, athletics, dance, music, etc.) usually have coaches. The coach's role is to

"Practice does not make perfect—it makes permanent."

observe the performance and provide the necessary feedback that allows the performers to systematically enhance what they do.

Like coaches, teachers of cognitive endeavors (yes, physical performances also require cognitive processing) need to provide observation and coaching. The difference between physical and cognitive activities is that physical errors are obvious: For example, when an athlete cannot dribble a basketball, it is apparent for all to see. With cognitive activities, such as division or transitional sentences, it is much less apparent when students do not understand. We only realize the errors when we have them use their new knowledge to solve problems or write an essay. In fact, many students have learned to cover up their ignorance and keep the teacher from finding out that they do not understand. Consequently, with cognitive activities, it is essential that we check students' understanding effectively during the initial stages of learning.

CHECKING FOR UNDERSTANDING

In most lessons, checking for understanding gives the teacher an idea of whether or not the students know what to do. The difference in knowing how something should be done and being able to do it is the quantum leap in learning. It is at this stage that we help students transition from knowing what to do (answering questions about which decisions have to be made and the criteria for those decisions) to applying that learning with teacher guidance. An essential consideration is determining the type and degree of guidance the students need based on the information gathered when checking for understanding.

When we teach how to write a topic sentence, we explain what a topic sentence is and what it does, and we show several examples of good topic sentences. We might then check to see if the students understand by having them explain what topic sentences are and what they do and possibly identify examples in well-written paragraphs, explaining why they are good topic sentences. This is typical of checking for understanding.

Combine Guided Practice With Checking for Understanding

When we move on to having students generate and write their own topic sentences, we need to provide guided practice, so their initial attempts are shaped and refined as necessary. This is the time to catch and correct errors in performance. The teacher might, in this case, provide two paragraphs without topic sentences and have the students generate possible topic sentences for each, then listen to the students share their examples, providing feedback (see the section "Knowledge of Results" in Chapter 3) about what is effective, what needs modifying, and how to modify it. The students might then be asked to write topic sentences for two additional paragraphs while the teacher circulates, examining the student writing. This gives teachers an additional opportunity to provide one-on-one assistance, if necessary. After the teacher is satisfied that the students are able to write effective topic sentences, the students may be asked to practice additional sentences independently.

For complex tasks, it may be desirable to guide students' initial practice on smaller pieces of learning. Consider the following examples:

- In history, we want students to learn to write a report, so we may have them practice generating subtopics for main topics or practice using online skills to research a variety of topics.

- In science, setting up complex lab equipment may need to be practiced with guidance before embarking on the actual experiment.

In each case, the teacher is ensuring that the initial practice with the material is guided. At any time, the teacher can intercede and provide additional information if necessary. As a result, errors (which will surely be made) will not be practiced, their detrimental effects on performance can be avoided, and unnecessary time won't be wasted in reteaching the material.

Chapter 12

Extending Your Students' Thinking

Guide for Group Discussion or Individual Study

Objectives:

Participants will:
a. Identify six levels of cognition.
b. Explain or describe each level in their own words.
c. Generate examples in their own content at all six levels.
d. Develop plans to extend students' thinking in subsequent classes.

Anticipatory Set:

Which one of each of the following pairs of questions requires more complex thinking? Why?
a. What did Columbus do?
b. Who was braver: Columbus or the first astronauts? Why?

a. Is this a restrictive or a nonrestrictive clause?
b. Write two sentences beginning with the words "The man . . . ". Complete one sentence with a restrictive clause and another sentence with a nonrestrictive clause.

a. Conduct the experiment outlined in the book.
b. Design an experiment to support or refute the hypothesis.

Input & Modeling:

Read the chapter "Extending Your Students' Thinking."

Checking for Understanding & Guided Practice:

List the six levels of thinking. Explain or describe each level. Generate examples or questions and activities in your own content at each level.

Develop plans to extend students' thinking in subsequent classes.

Independent Practice:

Monitor your future classes to make sure assignments require thinking beyond the level of basic comprehension.

Chapter 12

Extending Your Students' Thinking

The ability to think creatively, to solve problems, and to make satisfying and productive decisions is a fundamental goal of education. To help students achieve these goals, we need to become sensitive to, as well as learn how to elicit, higher levels of their thinking. One useful classification system of such thinking was developed by Benjamin Bloom (1956), who separated cognition into six levels: Knowledge, Comprehension, Application, Analysis, Synthesis, and Evaluation.

KNOWLEDGE

Possession of information, or knowledge, is the foundation from which all higher thinking grows. Think about a yik. "A what?" you ask. A yik. You can't think about it because you have no knowledge or information to indicate what a yik is or means. To think about it, you would need to get some information either directly through personal experience with a yik or vicariously through reading, observing, talking, or listening. Making information available to our students is so important to thinking that Chapter 5, "Providing Information Effectively," has been devoted to one method of accomplishing this purpose.

Questions from the teacher, from a text, or in a test that check whether a student possesses information require recall. Some examples of these items include the following:

- "Write the formula for _____."
- "Which countries did Napoleon conquer?"
- "Who wrote 'Ode on a Grecian Urn'?"
- "List the major wars in which the United States was involved."
- "State the rule for making these words plural."
- "Give the definition of _____."
- "Solve for x when $2x + 30 = 80$."

To answer each of these questions a student must recall or locate information but not necessarily understand that information.

COMPREHENSION

The second level of thinking is comprehension of the information that has been recalled or located. Information is not very useful unless it is understood. Suppose you received the information that a yik is a zuk. Now you can correctly answer the question "What is a yik?" by responding, "It's a zuk." But if you don't understand what a yik is, you don't know whether a yik is only one form of a zuk or whether you ride them or eat them. This may sound like a lot of nonsense to you, but that's the way content sounds to students when they don't understand it. A piece of information is like a brick. It's excellent material for future building, but it only clutters up your yard unless you understand how to make use of it.

> *"A piece of information is like a brick. It's excellent material for future building, but it only clutters up your yard unless you understand how to make use of it."*

Bits of information clutter up a student's mind unless that information is understood well enough to be used to build more complex concepts and generalizations. Sometimes teachers talk about students having a high TRI (trivia retention index) because they can recall a lot of information that they don't seem to understand. Consequently, that information is not useful to them. Their lack of understanding becomes obvious when we ask them to use that information to solve a problem, draw conclusions, or create a new hypothesis.

One way we can check whether students comprehend the information they possess is to have them state that information in their own words rather than recall what they have read or heard. Some examples include the following:

- "State in your own words some of the things
we discussed today."
- "Give your own definition of *persevere*."

Possible answer: "To persevere means that you make yourself keep on doing something even though, at times, you would like to stop."

- "Define *courage*."

Possible answer: "Courage means that you are afraid, but you make yourself go on as if you were not afraid."

- "Define *teaching*."

Possible answer: "Teaching is the process of examining what is to be learned and using the science of cause–effect relationships in learning, plus one's own artistry, to help students achieve that learning."

An additional way we can check students' comprehension is to have them give an example of the concept or generalization being learned, as in the following cases:

- "Give an example of a time when you persevered."

Possible answer: "I wanted to watch E.R. on TV, but I had a paper due, so I made myself keep writing until I finished. I persevered."

- "Give an example of courage."

Possible answer: "I remember one night when I was little, I heard noises and wanted to go into my parents' room, but I acted courageously. I pointed my flashlight out the window to scare the intruder and saw it was the wind blowing the tree branches against the window."

- "Give an example of a change in your teaching."

Possible answer: "Last year I thought my students should do research reports, so I assigned them. This year I am teaching them each skill: locating information, taking notes, organizing their notes, and writing the report's introduction, body, conclusion, bibliography, and so on. Instead of simply assigning them reports, I now am teaching how to do them."

When a student comprehends information, rather than merely recalling it, that information becomes useful in future problem solving or decision making; this in turn nurtures students' creative use of that information.

APPLICATION

Information and skills become useful when they can be applied to a situation one has never encountered. Generalizations can be used to solve new problems. Previous experience can be used to predict outcomes, estimate answers, extrapolate from data, and avoid errors. It is important that students have experience in applying what they learn to new problems or situations because it is only through experience that problem-solving skills predictably increase.

Familiarity

People who are good at something are people who perform that activity frequently. Experience that builds the patterns in the brain allows us to recognize different kinds of problems and to apply appropriate strategies in solving them. When one is inexperienced (in any area), one sees a situation in that area as unique. The more experiences one has, the greater the awareness of patterns in those experiences.

For example, if you are new to traveling by air, the airport is a novel environment, along with all of the procedures that occur there. If something goes wrong (missed or cancelled flight, lost luggage, etc.), you are hard-pressed to know what to do to solve it. After traveling a great deal, airports tend to blur, with only minor differences. Problems that were initially overwhelming are solved with very little thought or effort.

If we want students to be mathematical thinkers, then they need to be in a multitude of situations in which they have to think mathematically (i.e., solving real problems vs. using the same algorithm with different sets of numbers). If we want students to be good debaters, then they need to debate frequently. It is only when students are in educational settings that provide many procedural/problem-solving experiences that students truly develop proficient skills in those areas.

Applying Concepts in the Classroom

At the application level, most of the time we are looking for convergent thinking. You can bring together ideas and applications in the classroom, as in the following examples:

- "Using what you know about the plural form of words ending in *y*, make the following imaginary words plural: *zady, paisy*." (Note: If real words are used, such as *lady* and *baby*, the student may not be applying the rule but merely recalling correct spelling.)
- "If you wished to keep a liquid that is very similar to water from freezing, what might you add to it?"

- "Make sure you apply what you have learned about organizing notes to your term paper."
- "Locate the metaphors in the story."
- "In what way is our class a democracy? A dictatorship?"
- "There are twenty-eight people in this class. In how many different ways can they shake hands?"

The ability to apply a concept or a generalization to a new situation is the launching pad for all higher level thinking. Bloom (1956) separates advanced thinking into three levels. It is not essential that you are able to identify precisely which level you are encouraging or requiring of students. What is important is that you make sure students have information they understand and can apply before you expect them to achieve more complex cognitive feats.

ANALYSIS

Creative thinking and problem solving begin with analytic thinking: mentally taking something apart to better understand the relationship of the parts to each other and to the whole. Analysis may be accomplished using language, sonorous cues, or visual space. To analyze, you must be able to think categorically—that is, to organize and reorganize information into categories. Take a look at the following examples that require analysis:

- "In what ways is *Hamlet* typical of Shakespeare and in what ways is the play unique?"
- "Which factors do you believe contributed most to Edison's genius?"
- "On the basis of your observations, which variables could you eliminate as causal factors?"

Once students can take information apart to understand interrelationships, they are ready to reorganize that information into new patterns and apply creative skills to the information.

SYNTHESIS

The fifth category of complexity in thinking is synthesis or invention: the creation of something that is new to its creator. One difference between application and synthesis is that, usually, the former is convergent but the latter results from divergent thinking—something new and different. Note, however, that students can create only after they have skills and information, which can then be applied divergently to a new situation. Creativity does not spring from a vacuum but emerges from rigor and structure. The greatest artists spent countless hours developing comprehension and application in their discipline before the synthesis of masterpieces emerged.

All students have the potential for creative thinking. In many, that potential has been scientifically extinguished by their "majoring" in recalling the right answer, rather than using information as a launching pad for more complex thinking. Giving students the foundation for, and practice in, higher level thinking, plus rewarding that thinking (verbally, with extra credit, with a grade of *A*, with recognition) when it occurs, will encourage its frequency. The following instructions exemplify ways to get students to synthesize:

> *"Creativity does not spring from a vacuum but emerges from rigor and structure."*

- "Design your own experiment to demonstrate _____."
- "Create a hypothesis that would explain _____."
- "Write a poem or essay expressing your feelings about _____."
- "Invent a new way to _____."
- "Create a nonverbal statement (visual, auditory, kinesthetic, etc.) expressing _____."

EVALUATION

Evaluation, the making of judgments when there is no one right answer, is one of the most complex levels of thinking because evaluation is based on all other cognitive levels. Evaluation or judgment is essential to all intelligent and satisfying decisions.

When the criteria are known (e.g., "Identify the experiment that manipulates only one variable at a time."), learners simply apply those criteria to a new situation (application). If the criteria are not given (e.g., "Which research project do you consider to be better designed? Support your judgment."), learners must examine criteria from several categories and then select those that, in their judgment, are the most relevant to the particular situation.

The learners' values (intellectual, aesthetic, social, moral) are usually reflected in cognition at the level of evaluation. Questions that elicit value-based judgments might include the following:

- "Which poet did you enjoy more? Why?"
- "What do you believe was the person's most significant contribution? Support your answer."
- "Write three introductory paragraphs. Put a star by the one you think is best. State your reasons for selecting that paragraph."

We are tempted to believe that students who agree with us are good thinkers and that those who disagree are not. Note that, in evaluation, any judgment that can be supported is valid.

Performance at the evaluation level tightens students' thinking and opens them to the consideration of different points of view: a significant goal of education.

Remember, the important skill for you as a teacher is not to be able to classify the level of thinking of every assignment. Rather, you should be aware that the cognitive launching pad of knowledge and the comprehension that can be applied to new situations, plus your encouragement of higher levels of thinking, make it possible for students' minds to soar.

It is also helpful to keep this taxonomy in mind as you plan units of instruction. The initial stages of the unit can be designed to equip the students with the foundational knowledge they will later use in activities that require them to apply, analyze, synthesize, and evaluate. For students to achieve real understanding and use of information, they need experience using the upper levels of the taxonomy.

Chapter 13

Dignifying Errors to Promote Learning

Guide for Group Discussion or Individual Study

Objectives: *Participants will:*
1. Practice generating responses that
    a. Dignify an incorrect answer.
    b. Prompt the correct answer.
    c. Hold students accountable.

2. Use these techniques in subsequent class periods.

Anticipatory Set: If you asked the question, "Who was the first elected president of the U.S.?" and a student answered "Lincoln," how would you respond to that student?

Encourage a variety of responses by asking, "What is another possible response?"

Input & Modeling: Read the chapter "Dignifying Errors to Promote Learning."

Checking for Understanding & Guided Practice: List the three steps in correcting errors. Practice responding to incorrect answers, such as the following:

- "What is our national capital?"
  Answer: "New York."

- "What is a productive response to a student's error?"
  Answer: "You're wrong!"

- "Why are we reading these books?"
  Answer: "Because we have to."

Participants should recall incorrect answers they have encountered in their classes and generate a variety of teacher responses (there is no one right way) that dignify the incorrect answer, prompt the correct response, and hold the student accountable.

Independent Practice: Use this teaching technique in subsequent classes until it becomes automatic.

Chapter 13

Dignifying Errors to Promote Learning

There is one thing in teaching that you can bet will happen: Some students will produce incorrect answers. Unfortunately, in our society a wrong answer can become a put-down. Most of us dread appearing stupid or ignorant. Frequently, students will not participate or volunteer answers to avoid the risk (and humiliation) of being wrong. As a result, we may not have as much student participation in our class as we desire.

In this chapter, you will learn one way to deal with an incorrect answer, so the student will learn the correct response but will not feel "put down." How to do this is the science of effective teaching. How you do this is the art of effective teaching. If your teaching employs only science, you're a technologist. If your art does not have a scientific foundation, you're simply a promising amateur. You need both art and science to be a master teacher. Remember, the Taj Mahal is not a departure from the scientific principles of physics and engineering but an artistic manifestation of those principles.

"You need both art and science to be a master teacher."

MAKING EFFECTIVE USE
OF ERRONEOUS ANSWERS

When students give incorrect answers, there isn't just one thing they don't know; there are two:

1. They don't know the correct answer to the question.

2. They don't know the question to which their incorrect answer belongs.

Let's look at a very simple example. (Remember, first examples should be simple and unambiguous.)

Let's say you ask the question, "How much is five times seven?" and a student answers, "Thirty." The student doesn't know the facts $5 \times 7 = 35$ or $5 \times 6 = 30$. Consequently, there are two things that student needs to learn, not just one.

To teach both we must do the following:

a. *Dignify the student's response by supplying the question or statement to which the answer belongs.* You might say, "You would be right if I had asked five times six because five times six equals thirty. You are in the five times tables." Your comment tells the student, "You had something important to offer; you simply got it in the wrong place."

b. *Then, give the student an assist or prompt.* Remember, our function as teachers is to help students be right, not to catch them being wrong. An example of a prompt might be, "Suppose I ask you to buy six packages of gum for a nickel each. That would cost thirty cents. If you bought one more package for yourself, at a nickel per package, seven packages of gum would cost how much?" With that assistance, usually the student will respond, "Thirty-five cents."

c. *Finally, hold that student accountable.* It's important to assist the student, but it is equally important to insist that the student learn and remember. Consequently, we need to convey the message of accountability to the student. "Now, so that everyone remembers the answer, let's go over it again. How much is five times seven? And which number when multiplied by five equals thirty? I'll bet you'll remember that if I ask you the same question tomorrow." The unmistakable message is, "I expect you to."

COMMUNICATING ACCOUNTABILITY

Holding students accountable can be:

- *Gentle*—"Let's go over that one more time, so you remember it."
- *Medium*—"I'll check with you tomorrow to be sure you remember."
- *Unmistakable*—"You will be accountable for this on the test."

The measure of accountability is determined by the needs of the student for support in performance or demand for performance (for "patting" or "pitchforking").

Sample Student–Teacher Interactions

Frequently, students do not feel accountable. "Missed it, forget it" can become their creed. We change this attitude to "I'd better remember it" as we dignify students' incorrect responses, prompt the correct responses, and suggest that accountability for correct responses is expected in future encounters with the information. Look at the following sample interactions between a teacher and a student:

Teacher: "Is 'although, you have been studying' a dependent or independent clause?"

Student: "Independent."

Teacher: "If I had said, 'You have been studying,' that would be an independent clause because it could be a sentence. When it is preceded by *although*, it implies that something else is needed to finish it. It can't stand alone, so it is _____. Let's try another example, so it is clear to you."

Teacher: "What is the critical attribute of an argumentative essay?"

Student: "It gives information."

Teacher: "You're right that we must give information to persuade the reader that our point of view is correct. But if we only give information, we are writing an expository essay. What else do we intend to accomplish with our argument?"

Student: "Oh, we want to persuade the reader that our argument is correct."

Teacher: "Right, so when we only give information, we are writing what kind of essay? (*pauses*) And when our information is for the purpose of persuading the reader that our point of view is correct, we are writing what kind of essay? (*pauses*) Now you know the difference, and you shouldn't have any trouble with that on the exam."

Only rarely, if we think the student needs to experience failure, do we use the response "no" (e.g., "No, five times six is not thirty-five," "No, that is not an example of . . . ," "No, Napoleon did not . . . "). Be careful with the "no" that always wants to slip out of your mouth. It can be lethal and discourage students from further participation. When you hear an incorrect response, suppress your "no" unless you mean to use it deliberately.

Most of the time you will find that you can dignify students' incorrect responses, prompt them to correct answers, and hold them accountable, thereby encouraging comfortable, safe, and successful participation in your class.

DIGNIFYING DESPITE SETBACKS

At times, in spite of your prompt, a student may give a second incorrect answer. Again, you need to dignify the response by supplying the question or statement to which the second incorrect answer belongs. After doing so, move to a different student. (There's no point in mining for diamonds where none exist.) Then, you need to determine whether to go back to the original student to communicate that he or she is still accountable or to wait until later to go back privately. In either case, be sure you do go back, so students know they are responsible for learning.

Let's return to the example where the teacher asks a student to name the critical attribute of an argumentative essay. If the teacher's prompt for the answer "an attempt to persuade" fails, and instead the student offers "describes," a good response might be, "The author certainly needs to describe his or her point of view and the evidence to support it in an argumentative essay. All of that is for a certain purpose. Listen carefully, so you'll know that purpose." Then move on to a different student and go back either publicly or privately to the first student for repetition of the correct answer. "Because this is so important, we're going to go over it again."

Addressing Irrelevant Answers

At times, students may give completely irrelevant responses either because they are lost or because they want to shake up the class. If you believe the error is sincere and you can't think of any way to dignify it, you might say, "I'm not quite sure what you are thinking. Let's go on and see if it clears up for you." If you think the response is simply a bid for attention, it is best to ignore it and proceed to another student, so you don't give the clowning student the attention desired.

MAINTAINING DIGNITY ENABLES SUCCESS

In this chapter, we discussed ways of productively correcting errors in their simplest forms. Then, we introduced more complex forms and gave examples. Finally, we introduced the infrequent exception of it being occasionally correct to say, "No, you are wrong."

At first, using these techniques to deal with incorrect responses may seem cumbersome. "Who has time for all that?" you may ask. You will be surprised how automatic your enabling responses become as you practice using them with incorrect answers. There may be times when you tell a student, unequivocally, that he or she is wrong. Most students, however, will participate more enthusiastically and will venture more responses in your class if they know that not only will you maintain their dignity but that, in doing so, you'll also help them learn more and remember it longer—a major dividend from your skill in correcting incorrect answers.

Chapter 14

Using Time to Achieve More Learning

Guide for Group Discussion or Individual Study

Objectives:	*Participants will:* a. State several ways to use time that otherwise could be wasted. b. Design strategies employing these techniques for future classes.
Anticipatory Set:	Identify instances in your classes when time is wasted on matters that do not produce learning.
Input & Modeling:	Read the chapter "Using Time To Achieve More Learning."
Checking for Understanding & Guided Practice:	a. Identify three to five ways to increase learning by using class time that otherwise would be wasted. b. Apply these techniques to problems identified on your original list. c. Generate examples using these principles for your subsequent classes.
Independent Practice:	Try these techniques in subsequent classes to determine which are most effective.

Chapter 14

Using Time to Achieve More Learning

INCREASING LEARNING TIME

Time is the currency of teaching—what teachers have to spend to buy learning. Those of us teaching in the same school or district have the same amount to spend. We can invest time wisely in activities that result in students' learning, or we can fritter time away on inconsequential matters or in waiting for student readiness. Numerous studies have detailed how time is used in the classroom. The findings show tremendous variation in how teachers actually use the time allocated for instruction. In some classrooms, teachers use virtually all of it, giving their students the equivalent of weeks of additional learning time compared with classrooms that use time less effectively. For purposes of simplicity, we will look at how to increase time devoted to learning in three categories: before instruction, during instruction, and after instruction.

BEFORE INSTRUCTION

This category deals with the time that occurs during the transition at arrival time. This may be at the beginning of the day, the beginning of a period, or the beginning of a small-group activity in the classroom. Instructional activities cannot begin until all of the students are present. These transitions take time that can be put to productive use. There are a number of activities teachers can use to change the waiting time at arrival into learning time. However, it is necessary for these activities to be taught to the students, so the activities become part of the regular classroom procedure.

Write Directions on the Board or Overhead

As students enter the room, the first place their eyes should go is to the board or overhead to get directions as to what they need to do. Where do they need to be? What materials do they need to have? What do they need to do when they get there? For a high school calculus class, for example, you may write on the board, "Please get into groups of two. Open your book to the chapter on the natural log and differentiation. Read and discuss the various theorems and be ready to answer Questions 1 and 2." In a primary class, the directions might read, "Meet at the rug and practice reading the words on the board with a partner." Even kindergartners can be taught to follow pictures directing them to different tasks.

Receiving directions this way engages the students as soon as they arrive, instead of waiting with their minds out of gear. The students can pick up necessary materials on their way into the room and be ready to get to work much faster. This also eliminates having to quiet the class and get everyone's attention before beginning. In addition, you can use this initial time to take attendance or perform other administrivia while the students are productively engaged.

Engage Students in Sponge Activities

Sponge activities are learning activities that soak up precious time that would otherwise be lost. Sponge activities give students distributed practice in using or applying past learnings while they are waiting for all of the students to arrive.

Sponge activities have two characteristics:

1. They are activities that accommodate late arrivals or early departures.

Late-arriving students must be able to catch on quickly to what is happening when they enter the room. Also, when you do not dismiss the whole class as a group but "spin" students off in small groups to eliminate traffic jams at materials centers, the sponge activity must not penalize the early departures.

2. Sponge activities are used to review or practice something already known.

These activities should not be used to introduce new concepts or material to the students. Rather, they are an excellent way of providing practice sessions that are short, massed or distributed, and intense. They facilitate fast learning and long remembering (see Chapter 10, "Practice Doesn't Make Perfect").

While waiting for all students to arrive, consider writing directions on the board or posing activities such as the following to the students already present:

- Be ready to state three of the important differences we discussed yesterday between the continental shelf and the deep water of the ocean.
- Be ready to give the correct verb form for the following sentences.
- Show me with a bent finger if this noun needs an apostrophe to show possession or not. Form a zero to show me it's not.
- There are two guide words on the board. Using a finger to point, does the word I say come before this page of the dictionary, on the same page, or after this page? (*Practice several words.*)
- Give me as many synonyms as you can think of for the word _____.
- Take the number five. Double it. Double it. Subtract three. Subtract two. Divide by three. What do you have? (*Do several of these—longer, shorter, easier, or more complex depending on your students.*)
- Be ready to identify the author of this line and discuss its meaning in the text: "It is a far, far better thing that I do, than I have ever done."
- Show me the answer to this equation: $3 + 5 =$ _____." (*Practice several equations.*)

Verbal or written responses, which the teacher can walk around the room to examine, give an immediate assessment of what is understood and remembered and what needs to be retaught (with no papers to correct!).

Ask Questions to Get Everyone Thinking

While taking roll or passing out papers and materials, ask a question of the group. Give students time to think about the answer as you take roll or return papers. Then, call on a student you believe will answer correctly. This gives everyone the right answer to check against their own, and corrections can be made without public disclosure of error. If appropriate, ask the student who answered, or another student, to supply the reason for the validity of the answer.

During this time, you can be taking care of administrative tasks. Asking additional questions, giving thinking time, and then calling on students for answers can give you whatever time is necessary for your administrative chores. Meanwhile, the students are engaged in thinking and learning.

Spin Off Students at the End of Class

When dismissing students or sending them to gather materials, do so without creating a traffic jam by beginning an activity and spinning off a few students at a time. Here are some examples of ways to spin off students:

- "While table one gets materials, let's review the essential steps in the experiment."
- "Explain what you're to do with your neighbor and dismiss each other to get your materials."
- "Be ready to tell the introductory sentence for your essay as I dismiss your writing group."
- "Signal me when you have decided on the three colors (or events, characters, problem, resolution, etc.) you will use, and I'll excuse you."

Make the Most of Sponge Activities

You may notice that many of the techniques for engaging all of the students in thinking are similar to those used for checking for understanding when introducing new material (see Chapter 9, "Checking Your Students' Understanding"). The intent of these techniques is the same in both cases: engage the minds of all students—not just the few who usually volunteer—in processing and practicing the material.

Use of inevitable waiting time for learning is limited only by your knowledge of what your class needs to practice or extend and your creativity. What your class needs to practice is what you use to develop your sponge activities. Remember that the attributes of an effective practice session are that it is short and intense, with the intent to learn. These activities also mass the students' practice (i.e., several examples are practiced in a

> *"Time is the currency of teaching. That's what teachers have to spend to 'buy' learning."*

short time) at the beginning stages of learning and distributed to promote long-term retention. You'll find sponge activities fit those qualities very well. The students are engaged, the activities are quick, and the novelty of the format often increases student interest.

It is amazing how much students' memory and learning can be increased through the use of sponge activities. Depending on your upcoming instruction, these directions or sponge activities may become the anticipatory set for that instruction.

DURING INSTRUCTION

One would obviously think that the period when students spend the most time on learning is during instruction. In reality, that depends completely on the quality of the instruction or activity. Following are some areas that can be examined to see if we are getting the maximum benefit of our teaching time.

Task Difficulty

For maximum engagement, the level of difficulty of what we are having the students do must be correct. In the given curricular area, where does their prior learning leave off and new learning need to begin? At this point the level of task difficulty is correct.

Students who are given work that they find unchallenging often spend much time off task doing other things, most of which we would rather they not do. If the task is too difficult, then obviously the students cannot engage in it and, again, tend to wander off into other activities. Task difficulty for instruction (which, of course, varies with the learner's previous experience in that type of task) maximizes engagement when students correctly respond about 75% of the time. For reading and comprehension tasks, students should be able to decode the material with about 90–95% accuracy for high engagement and comprehension.

Meaning and Interest

The more meaningful and interesting the learning is to the student, the more time the student will spend being engaged in the learning. Meaning and interest are not the same thing. Meaning is a connection to the learner's experience or relevance to the learner. Interest may accompany this or may be elicited by the novelty of something that has little or no meaning to the learner. See the chapters on motivation (Chapters 2 and 3) and making material meaningful (Chapter 8) for techniques to increase both of these factors in your teaching.

Questioning and Responding

In most classrooms, we spend time asking questions (posing problems, etc.) and having students respond to those questions. What is the student engagement rate in these activities? It depends on how they are done. For maximum learning during these times, we want every student answering every question and solving every problem. This is the opposite of having a few students answer the questions or solve the problems with the assumption (often incorrect) that the rest of the students will learn by watching.

Ask Questions of the Group

Beam your question to the entire group so that every student feels the responsibility to formulate an answer. Avoid naming a student and then asking the question, which frequently results in only the designated student thinking while the rest leave their minds in neutral. You can visually see this happen when you name the student and ask a question. You can then watch all of the other students look at the designated student with no intent to formulate an answer themselves. You may know whom you want to answer before asking the question, but still ask the question of the group so they all will think.

Use Wait Time After Asking a Question

In our culture, we tend to be uncomfortable with silence and want to fill it. An effective teacher needs to know how to use silence productively. Ask a question and wait a period of time before calling on anyone. It takes time to think, and allotting wait time after asking a question allows all students time to formulate an answer—and possibly edit the answer they think of to make it better.

Having students visibly indicate when they have an answer will let you see the number of students ready to answer and help you gauge your wait time. For example, you might say, "Raise your hand when you can tell me how the main character justified her actions" or "I'll know you're ready to give me an example of being garrulous when your eyes are on me." When wait time becomes a regular part of your teaching practice, the amount of time you need to wait will decrease. The students learn they will be accountable for participating and, as a result, will get in gear more quickly.

Make Your Questions Directives Instead of Pleas

To maximize learning time for all students, optimally we will have planned to deliver curriculum that is meaningful, engaging, and worthwhile for the students. We also need to create an expectation that all students put forth effort toward their own growth. That expectation can often be communicated in the way we ask students questions or pose problems.

An atmosphere of volunteerism (and possibly a resultant low expectation for student engagement) is created when we plea for participation. Questions begun with "Who would like to . . . ?," "Would someone please read . . . ?" or "Can someone please tell us . . . ?" unintentionally send the message that whoever wants to participate may, but everyone is not expected to. To set the expectation that everyone needs to expend effort, we should make our questions directives, such as the following:

- "Be ready to . . . "
- "All of you think to yourself how you would define . . . "
- "You need to come up with an example. Raise your hand when you're ready to share yours."
- "On a piece of scratch paper, write down a formula for finding . . . "

The message we're communicating is "I expect everyone to think and participate." We want to create an environment in which we insist students put forth effort to learn. At the same time, we must make sure they know that we will assist them in being successful. When the learning task is at the correct level of difficulty, this is a reasonable expectation.

Have All Students Respond to Questions

Once you have everyone thinking, it is also beneficial to maximize their ability to respond. Not only is it gratifying to students to be able to share the results of their thinking, but it also may provide valuable assessment data for you. Choral responses, signaled responses, individual written responses, and individual public responses (see Chapter 9, "Checking Your Students' Understanding," for more details) increase students' ability to share the results of their thinking. Such techniques not only stimulate each student to answer every question and solve every problem, but they also give the teacher essential data about who knows what, whether the majority is certain or uncertain, and whether material is understood or needs to be retaught.

AFTER INSTRUCTION

To maximize learning time after the instructional activity, we want to look closely at what we have the students do. Often, teachers assign practice so that the students increase their facility and fluency with the skills or concepts they are learning. The quality of this practice determines the amount of learning that occurs as a result. Teachers assign two kinds of practice: rehearsal and elaboration.

Rehearsal

Rote or identical practice, or doing the same thing repeatedly, is rehearsal. This is shallow processing. We assign rehearsal practice for skills we want the students to memorize, so they have high-speed recall. Skills such as math facts, spelling words, sight words, and vocabulary fit into this category. The most effective activity for this type of skill is the intense practice of a small amount of material (three to five pieces of information) for a short amount of time (see Chapter 10, "Practice Doesn't Make Perfect"). This type of material tends to be discrete, unrelated bits of information (e.g., one spelling word has no relation to another).

When we have students practice too much material at once, it overloads working memory. When teachers put too much in, something falls out (figuratively speaking). As a result, when students practice fifteen spelling words or all of the multiplication facts for seven, for example, they learn very little. It is much more effective is to practice three to five of them for a while, and then do something else, returning later for additional short practices. It is only when those three to five items are in long-term memory that teachers can add new material.

Elaboration

Connecting new material to something already understood is elaboration. This is deep processing. Concepts and generalizations are best internalized when connected to information already in the learner's long-term memory. The greater the number of connection points, the more readily the material will be learned. For example, notice the number of different points of connection for involving all students in thinking during a lesson: anticipatory set, checking for understanding, group and independent practice, sponge activities, and meaning. Having so many points of connection increases the probability of learning, and using these techniques enhances your instruction. Have the students practice this type of material by:

Paraphrasing—Have students put information into their own words.

- "Tell why the main character chose to solve the problem in the way he did."
- "Explain how you determined that the probability of the outcome was . . . "
- "How do supply and demand affect the pricing of materials?"

When students must explain in their own words, they have to process the information and integrate it with what they already know.

Summarizing—Have students distill the most important ideas or events in the material.

- "Write a summary of the concepts and relationships we worked on in math today."
- "In your groups, you discussed the questions I gave you. Work with your group to create an outline of that material."
- "Write what happened in the beginning, middle, and end of the story."
- "We've been discussing international conflicts in which our country has been engaged. Tell me, which are some attributes that they all share?"

These summarizing types of activities require the students to internalize and process the information. They also require thinking and use of language.

Giving Personal Examples—Have students generate an example of the concept or generalization from their own life.

- "Describe a time when someone was pedantic with you."
- "Give an example of supply and demand in your own household."
- "Write down a situation when it would be helpful to make a function chart for yourself."

Again, this activity requires the learner to process and understand the material to link it to something that is already in long-term memory. The quality of this type of practice helps ensure that when the students are working alone or in groups, independent of the teacher, they are maximizing their learning time, not just keeping busy.

When students function independently of the teacher, the skills they have in self-direction and problem solving also determine how much of their time is devoted to learning. (See Chapter 17, "Teaching for Independent Learning," to enhance these skills in your students.)

USING YOUR CREATIVITY

Obviously, the most important way to reap learning dividends from time expended is by excellence in teaching. If, in addition, you use techniques (sponge activities, assessment, effective questioning and practice) that take advantage of otherwise wasted learning time, you will encourage students' maximum involvement and accomplishment in learning. Use your own creativity to tailor these techniques to your content, thereby increasing learning time in your classroom.

Chapter 15

Teaching So Students Remember

Guide for Group Discussion or Individual Study

Objectives: *Participants will:*
a. Recall five factors that affect students' ability to remember what they have learned.
b. Generate examples using each factor in subsequent classes.
c. Practice incorporating principles of retention in future plans for teaching.

Anticipatory Set: List some techniques you use to help students remember what they have learned in your class.

Input & Modeling: Read the chapter "Teaching So Students Remember."

Checking for Understanding & Guided Practice:
a. List the five factors that promote information retention and examine your original list for examples of each.
b. Generate examples for any factor you omitted in your original list.
c. Develop examples of specific ways you can incorporate these principles in subsequent classes.

Independent Practice: Incorporate principles of retention in future classes. Determine which ones are most effective. Describe to your students what you are doing and encourage them to use these same techniques in their independent study.

Chapter **15**

Teaching So Students Remember

Allll of us have suffered the fallout of forgetting something we wanted to remember. We've also listened with dismay as our students assured us, "We've never learned that!" when we distinctly remember teaching it.

Many factors that are beyond our control affect students' memory, and no one can guarantee remembering. There are, however, five factors we can incorporate in our teaching to substantially increase the probability that students will remember what they have learned in our classes.

FIVE TEACHING PRINCIPLES TO PROMOTE RETENTION

Many of these factors for teaching excellence are discussed in other chapters of this book. Excellence in instruction not only increases motivation to learn, but it also increases the speed of learning and the probability of retention. Consequently, this chapter is a useful review of many of the techniques you've already learned, and, as a result, your own memory of those techniques should increase.

Meaning

One of the most important factors that influences remembrance of academic content, skills, or processes is the degree of meaning that particular learning had for the student. Chapter 8, "Making Material Meaningful," stressed the importance of using experiences from students' lives to illustrate the concept or generalization being taught. If instruction in that chapter was effective, and if the examples were meaningful, you will remember that meaning is not inherent in material. Rather, meaning exists in the relationship of that material to students' own knowledge and past experience. When material is meaningful, students not only learn it more rapidly but they also remember it for longer periods of time (see Box 15.1).

Box 15.1   Tailor Your Teaching to Your Audience

Would you vary how you taught the concept of 200 feet, depending on your students? Take a look at the following ways in which teachers might present 200 feet in a meaningful way:

- For Hawaiian students, the teacher might say, "Suppose you rode your surfboard 200 feet."
- For students in Colorado, a teacher might say, "Suppose you skied 200 feet down a slope."
- For students in Iowa, a teacher might say, "Suppose you planted 200 feet of corn."
- For football players, a teacher might say, "Suppose the gridiron were shortened to 200 feet."

The effective teacher takes the essence of what is being taught and translates it into students' knowledge and past experience. The example not only makes the material more meaningful, but it also provides a reference point that helps the students recall the material when it is needed.

Meaningful Examples

Let's say you're trying to teach your students how to write an argumentative essay. You would probably get them interested in learning by saying, "Suppose you wrote an argumentative essay to persuade me not to give a final exam. Let's look at the elements you would need to include." This gets students' attention because who wouldn't want to know the way to get out of having to take a final? The information will be internalized because it could concretely affect the students' lives. As a result, teaching in this way enables students to reach into their memory banks at a future time for the reference point—"Oh yes, those were the elements that we included in our argument against the teacher giving a final."

Recall our dessert example from Chapter 8. It might be effective to tell your students, "You can remember that *dessert* is spelled with two *s*'s because if you eat too much dessert, you'll get bigger around your middle. *Dessert* has more *s*'s in its middle." This way of teaching brings something students already know to the current learning and gives them a reference point when they have to discriminate between *dessert* and *desert*.

> *"Excellence in instruction not only increases motivation to learn, but it also increases the speed of learning and the probability of retention."*

In each of these examples, something the student already knows or has experienced is brought forward by the teacher and connected to the new learning to be acquired. Old learning transfers from the past to the present and assists not only the speed of acquisition but also the appropriate transfer of that new learning into a future situation when it is needed. You'll learn more about how to accomplish this transfer in Chapter 16, "Teaching for Transfer."

Feeling Tone

A second factor that promotes retention is feeling tone. We remember those things with which pleasant and unpleasant feelings are associated. When feelings are neutral (i.e., when the event doesn't make any difference), then it frequently doesn't make any difference if you remember it, so you don't. That material is forgotten.

Pleasant Feeling Tone

We hope you remember, from the chapters on motivation, that pleasant feeling tones increase the learning effort that students put forth. Pleasant feeling tones also increase the probability that what was learned will be remembered. That is why we should try to make our classes pleasant and interesting and our students successful.

Unpleasant Feeling Tone

Sometimes, we may want to interrupt pleasant feelings to raise students' level of concern about the importance of learning and remembering certain material that they will need in the future. Consequently, we introduce slightly unpleasant feeling tones. An excellent example of the function of unpleasant feeling tones in retention is the wise—not sadistic—use of tests.

Tests frequently are accompanied by the unpleasant feeling of anxiety due to accountability and evaluation. As a result, tests can be an important aid to retention, particularly if they're given regularly (so no one test is a life or death matter) and if students get immediate feedback (knowledge of results), so they know if their answers are correct or incorrect and why.

Making the effort to recall material is one of the best ways to practice that material. As a result, tests contribute a great deal to retention because they cause students to exert maximum effort to recall. Many short quizzes, only occasionally collected by the teacher, give a great deal of highly motivated practice and let students know what they have achieved and what they need to study.

When the consequences of a test are so anxiety evoking that the student must use excessive energy to deal with the anxiety, there is little energy left for remembering. Those excessive feelings of concern may result in a test-phobic student who knows the material but can't remember it. Sometimes, to protect themselves, students need to deny the importance of the test and put forth no effort whatsoever to dilute unpleasant feelings until they become neutral. Neutral feeling tones may relieve tension, but they do nothing for retention. Remember, if "it doesn't matter," it usually won't be remembered.

For maximum retention, students need to associate material and processes with pleasant feelings. Unpleasant feelings also are powerful, but they can have dangerous side effects. Neutral feeling tones are of no aid to retention.

Degree of Original Learning

A third factor that increases the probability of retention is students' ability to achieve a high degree of original learning. We've all had the experience of meeting people and two minutes later, when we need to introduce them, find we've forgotten their names because we didn't pay attention and learn them well in the first place.

Our teaching responsibility is to provide students with the opportunity to achieve a degree of learning high enough to prevent material from being easily forgotten. (Not all students avail themselves of that opportunity, but if we don't provide it, the fault is ours.) In Chapter 9, "Checking Your Students' Understanding," we suggest ways

"Don't just cover material. If you do, use a shovel, cover the material with dirt, and lay it to rest, for it will be dead as far as memory is concerned."

to ensure a firm foundation, so learning is retained. Every chapter in this book should help you teach in a way that contributes to that foundation of learning.

One caution to be sounded is don't just cover material. If you do, use a shovel, cover the material with dirt, and lay it to rest, for it will be dead as far as memory is concerned. If you don't have time to teach everything well, teach the most important concepts or processes for a high degree of learning. If you must, assign the rest of the material to your students for independent learning (homework); in this way, what may not be learned well is the least important material.

Schedule of Practice

Simply because students learn something one day you well know that there is no guarantee they will remember it next week—that is, unless we incorporate in our instructional plan the power of a deliberate schedule of practice to achieve retention.

Mass First, Then Distribute

From Chapter 10, "Practice Doesn't Make Perfect," you might remember that massing practice (i.e., providing many short, intense practice periods close together) makes for fast learning and a high degree of original learning. However, even though something may be well learned, if it is not used, it can be forgotten. Consequently, once something has been learned, we need to increase the probability of its retention by changing the practice schedule from massed to distributed. Distributed practice means that material is periodically reviewed but with longer and longer time intervals between reviews. Distributed practice makes for durable learning that is forgetting resistant.

We frequently assume that our students are conscientious and will distribute their own practice by doing homework or rereading or reviewing material. If we explain to them why this is necessary for ensuring they remember what they have learned, and we also occasionally model the value of distributed practice by reviewing material in class, students will be more likely to assume responsibility for their own distributed practice.

Use Optimal Practice Time

Use bits of time in your class to review previous learning. For example, while your class is assembling or preparing to leave, when you're passing back or collecting papers, or when you have unavoidable delays (e.g., the projector bulb burned out or you're waiting for a speaker, a film, a bell, students to arrive), practice something that needs periodic review. Chapter 14, "Using Time to Achieve More Learning," suggests several ways to use those bits of time for distributed practice. By doing so, you will make a major contribution to your students' ability to remember.

So far, you have read about four factors you can use to increase students' retention of what they have learned: meaning, feeling tone, degree of original learning, and practice schedule. These factors are not discrete; they interact. We separate them only to bring each to your attention. By deliberately incorporating each factor in your teaching, you can contribute immeasurably to your students' success at remembering what they have learned.

Transfer

The last factor that can promote or interfere with retention is the phenomenon of transfer of learning. When transfer facilitates learning, past learning transfers to the present and not only facilitates present learning but also provides a springboard for all future problem solving, decision making, and creativity. Be aware, though, that transfer can also hinder the acquisition of new learning. When transfer interferes with new learning, past learning transfers to the present and blocks retrieval of something you wish to remember. For example, you may keep recalling your friend's maiden name when you want to remember her married name.

Transfer is so important that the next chapter focuses on the ways you can encourage transfer. By deliberately using teaching principles that promote transfer, you can take what you have learned in this book and transfer that learning to your increasingly effective future teaching.

Chapter 16

Teaching for Transfer

Guide for Group Discussion or Individual Study

Objectives:	*Participants will:* a. Identify four factors that promote transfer. b. Generate examples using those factors in their own content area. c. Plan for future class sessions that make use of transfer theory.
Anticipatory Set:	What factors in teaching promote transfer of learning to new situations?
Input & Modeling:	Read the chapter "Teaching for Transfer."
Checking for Understanding & Guided Practice:	a. Identify four factors that promote transfer. b. Recall examples of errors that result when students perceive things as similar, and develop discriminators that emphasize differences. c. Generate examples that emphasize similarity of students' previous knowledge to new learnings in subsequent classes. d. Identify associations students bring to your content area. Develop ways of changing nonproductive associations and strengthening productive ones. e. Develop a guide in which you rate adequate degrees of original learning. Determine how you will secure evidence that your students have achieved that level of learning. f. Identify critical attributes of subsequent instructional content and determine how your students will identify and learn those attributes.
Independent Practice:	Try these ideas in subsequent classes and identify those ideas that are most productive. Remember, an excellent idea or technique often needs modification and polishing before it becomes an element of artistic teaching.

Chapter **16**

Teaching for Transfer

THE POWER OF TRANSFER

Transfer is one of the most powerful principles of learning. Transfer occurs when past learning influences the acquisition of new learning. Transfer is the basis of all creativity, problem solving, and decision making. In addition to these important functions, transfer can dramatically shorten or lengthen the time it takes to acquire new learning.

The Premier Predictor

Transfer predicts the speed at which students acquire new learning more reliably than IQ. Think of a student who spends most of his or her time reading *Road and Track* or under the hood of a car, tearing down the engine. Now think of another student with the same IQ who spends most of his or her time reading Shakespeare. Which student will more rapidly learn the fuel injection system of a new automobile? It's obvious, isn't it? Suppose the first student had the lower IQ. Would you change your opinion? Of course not. It's also obvious that the second student would more rapidly learn the meaning of English words of the sixteenth century, not because the student is brighter but because the student already has a wealth of previous learning that can transfer to the new learning task.

Positive Transfer

In a similar way, Edison, Michelangelo, and the first astronauts to land on the moon acquired a great deal of knowledge and skill to transfer into their performance. Certainly, ability played a role in their success, but other humans of equal ability could not have achieved in the same way unless they also had the prerequisite learning necessary for the transfer that made achievement possible. This process of old learning accelerating the acquisition of new learning is called positive transfer.

Negative Transfer

Transfer of old learnings is not always positive. Old learnings can interfere with the acquisition of new learning and result in confusion or errors. When old learning interferes with new learning, it is called negative transfer. For example, once you have learned to pronounce the English word *robe*, it is more difficult to pronounce that word correctly when you see it written in the French sentence "C'est une robe." Think about grammar, too. Because students learn that an apostrophe can indicate possession, that knowledge may transfer negatively and result in their writing "It's leg was broken." If previous teachers required students to memorize and regurgitate material, it is more difficult to encourage students to do their own thinking rather than parrot what previous teachers said.

> "Transfer occurs when past learning influences the acquisition of new learning. Transfer is the basis of all creativity, problem solving, and decision making."

Effectively Hooking the Past Into the Present

To use the learning propulsion from positive transfer and minimize the interference of negative transfer, it is important to identify the factors that stimulate transfer. In our teaching, we should then deliberately incorporate those factors that facilitate student learning and performance and eliminate or minimize those that could cause interference.

Diagrammatically expressed, we can affect only the present, but in that present we can hook into past learning experiences and pull that learning forward to facilitate present learning (see Figure 16.1). We "cut it off" to prevent the interference of negative transfer. We teach to increase the positive transfer of present learning to future situations where it is appropriate and minimize negative transfer to a future situation where that learning would be inappropriate.

Figure 16.1   The Path of Effective Transfer

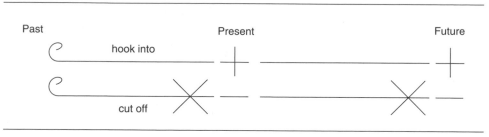

PROMOTING TRANSFER

Four factors in a learning situation can promote transfer. No one is most important, and often they operate in concert. By becoming aware of each of them, we can enhance positive transfer and minimize negative transfer as we teach.

1. Similarity

Whenever two learnings have an element or elements that appear to the learner as similar, it is more probable that one learning will transfer into the other. The similarity may be perceived in:

- the environment.
- the way the learner feels or thinks.
- the mode of attack or learning methodology being employed.

When a student learns to use the library to locate material for an English class, those skills will likely transfer into the new task of locating material for a science class. Even though the content is different, the perception of the library as a source of information and the mode of attack are the same.

Perceptions of similarity can also lead to negative transfer. Twins are perceived as similar, so one twin might be mistakenly called by the other's name. Students confuse *mitosis* and *miosis* and *latitude* and *longitude* because of similarity.

Transfer of Thoughts and Feelings

The ways in which we feel or think also transfer. Notice the feelings you transfer from your past to the present when you read these chapters. Some of you are transferring feelings of "I always wanted to know more about how to teach effectively." Others are transferring (with a groan) feelings of, "Great, something else I have to learn" or "Who doesn't know that?" Some of you are transferring your typical style of thinking analytically. Others are transferring their more holistic style and are concerned that analytic thinking may destroy creativity.

An English professor and a statistician would transfer different ways of thinking to their reading of a research article in a professional journal. The statistician would be looking at the validity with which results had been interpreted and could be substantiated. The English professor would probably be thinking about organization, clarity of presentation, and word usage.

Students transfer previous ways of thinking into their present classes. When a course requires a very different way of thinking, changing from analytic to holistic, from concrete to abstract, from one right answer to many different answers, from one way of organizing language to a new way, negative transfer can result from the similarity. The old mode of thinking or feeling transfers into and interferes with new performance expectations.

On the other hand, once a student learns how to think analytically, that skill does not have to be relearned for the next class that requires it. Once a student has learned to deal productively with abstractions, that thinking skill can be transferred to new situations that are perceived as similar.

Using Similarity for Positive Transfer

Sometimes the similarity of the past learning to the present is in the mode of attack. "Can you remember?" elicits the behavior of reaching into a memory bank, a strategy different from the response to "Can you figure out?" or "Could you possibly imagine?"

Because similarity promotes transfer, we need to emphasize that similarity when the transfer will be positive. For example, you could inform students that the French word for *red* is *rouge*, which is the same word we use for the red color women put on their cheeks and lips. By saying, "This problem is similar to the one you handled so effectively last week," you could encourage a perplexed student to transfer successful problem-solving skills.

If the similarity will promote negative transfer, we should keep the two learnings separate. Don't teach *latitude* and *longitude* on the same day. When two learnings become confused, we emphasize the difference. For example, you might tell students that unlike in English, the modifier comes after the noun in French. We say *red hat*; unlike us, the French say *chapeau rouge*.

There is no way that this short chapter can explore all of the possibilities for eliciting positive transfer and minimizing negative transfer as a result of similarity of two learnings. I hope that your reading will generate enough interest so that looking for similarities will transfer into continuing investigation of their potential in teaching effectiveness.

2. Association

Whenever two events, feelings, or actions occur at the same time, they can become associated—bonded or welded together—so the presence of one elicits the recall of the other. *Romeo* elicits *Juliet*. *Statistics* usually elicits the feeling "never again." *Pavlov* elicits *conditioning*. Even though there is no similarity between the two items, they have occurred together, so they become associated.

This bonding is especially powerful for feelings that have become associated with concepts or environments. Look at the feelings you have bonded to the concepts of terrorism, motherhood, slums, science, poetry, and final exams. Because of the transfer power of such association, we want to bond our content and classroom experiences with students' feelings of interest, competence, and successful achievement. As a result, meeting that content in the future will elicit feelings of competence and enjoyment. This book was produced to facilitate the bonding of your efforts to become increasingly effective with the satisfaction derived from your students' accelerated achievement.

Simulating for Association

Simulation is one way of increasing students' perception of similarity and bonding appropriate actions to significant cues in the environment. Fire drills use the similarity of an auditory signal, regardless of the difference of other factors in the environment, and bond that signal to the response of an orderly evacuation. Simulations at the NASA Space Center transferred to the completely new experience of a near perfect moon landing. As we anticipate skills and information needed by our students in future situations, simulations of those situations (interviews, experiments, examinations, problem situations) will increase the probability that what we are teaching will transfer appropriately into the future.

Using Personal Experience

We also need to use examples from the students' own experiences, emphasizing the similarity of what they already know, understand, and have experienced, so it will transfer approximately to new learning. For example, if we're teaching base six in math (heaven knows why), we can hook into students' knowledge of soft drinks and use as examples single cans, six packs, and a carton of six six packs. The selection of the examples we use is such a powerful propellant to learning that Chapter 8, "Making Material Meaningful," is devoted to that important element of effective teaching.

3. Degree of Original Learning

If something is worth teaching, it is worth teaching well. While achieving an adequate degree of learning is the responsibility of the learner, contributing to that adequacy is a primary responsibility of the instructor. This book was produced to help you fulfill that responsibility.

Well-Learned Information Transfers Best

Information that is well learned will transfer more appropriately into the future than will poorly or insufficiently learned skills or material. Clearly, a student who barely understands the scientific process is not going to perform acceptable research. The student who has just begun to work with clay will not produce a masterpiece. The student who is a beginner in basketball will not

> *"If something is worth teaching, it is worth teaching well."*

score the most points. These students have not acquired a high enough degree of learning to transfer their skills dependably and predictably into future successful performances.

Aiding Transfer When Information Has Not Been Well Learned

Transfer is not always within our control. However, with careful planning (plus scientific and artistic instruction), we can identify when similarities will contribute to positive transfer and emphasize differences when we do not wish that transfer to occur. Effective and artistic teaching also increases the probability that your students' interest and success will become associated with your subject field, and a higher degree of learning will be achieved. Still, there are factors beyond our control that also can influence the perception of similarity, association, and degree of learning. A student may perceive some element of our class as similar to something that caused him or her difficulty in the past. Also absence or lack of effort or aptitude can result in an inadequate degree of learning.

4. Critical Attributes

There is a fourth factor that promotes positive transfer and that is completely within our control—identification of the critical attribute that makes something what it is. When students understand the critical attributes of learned material, appropriate transfer of current learning into future situations is virtually guaranteed.

Critical attributes are those attributes that differentiate one thing from another. A critical attribute of a mammal is that it has mammary glands. There are other attributes possessed by mammals, such as being warm-blooded and having an internal skeleton, but those attributes do not distinguish mammals from birds or reptiles. A critical attribute of a topic sentence is that it presents the generalization that all the other sentences support or develop. It has other essential elements, such as a subject and a predicate, but those do not distinguish it from other sentences.

Teaching These Critical Attributes

The power of a critical attribute is that, once identified, it can be applied to any new situation to confirm or deny the applicability of previous knowledge to that new, never-before-encountered situation. This application is the launching pad for problem solving, decision making, and creativity.

While we may encourage students to discover critical attributes, most of the time we should plan to teach those attributes and let students' discovery be the identification of those attributes in new situations.

To teach a critical attribute we need to

1. *Identify the attribute that makes something what it is.* Identifying critical attributes is not always an easy task, and, in some cases, it's not even possible. However, it is our responsibility to identify and teach these attributes as best we can. For example, which attributes differentiate explorers from conquerors, pioneers, trespassers, and nosy people? Common attributes could be curiosity, initiative, courage, fortitude, and perseverance. However, the critical attributes are as follows:

- Explorers penetrate unknown areas.
- Explorers' actions are condoned by the society in which they live.
- Explorers search primarily to secure information.

These three critical attributes eliminate conquerors (primary purpose is conquest), people who are lost (primary purpose is to get back home), and trespassers and nosy persons (not condoned by their society).

2. *Cite simple and obvious examples.* Make sure you carefully select examples in advance. Don't ask students for examples when you introduce a critical attribute. Students have an absolute gift for volunteering murky or confusing examples or those that present an exception to the rule. Instead, inform students that Columbus was an explorer because he was seeking information as to whether a vessel could arrive in the East by sailing west, a voyage his society sanctioned. Napoleon, on the other hand, was not an explorer because even though he went into lands new to him, his primary purpose was conquest, not information.

3. *Cite more complex examples.* When your checking for understanding reveals that students have grasped the basic idea, it is good to move on to more involved examples, fairly testing their knowledge and

understanding. You could continue teaching about attributes of explorers and exploration with the following information: "The U.S. astronauts were funded by their country to explore the surface of the moon, record data, and bring back specimens for scientific investigation; however, their voyage also fulfilled the purpose of demonstrating the scientific supremacy of the United States." Only after students can apply the critical attribute to discriminate between simple and then more complex exemplars and nonexemplars should they be encouraged to generate their own examples.

4. *Have students generate examples.* At this point, students should be ready to transfer their knowledge into the generation of examples that do and do not satisfy the criteria set by the critical attributes. This process should increase the probability that, in the future, they will be able to transfer the discriminator, skill, concept, or generalization approximately to new learning, problem solving, decision making, and creative endeavors.

5. *Teach the limits of critical attributes.* Aggravating exceptions to rules, generalizations, categories, and critical attributes seem to emerge just when we think we truly understand. It seems that the critical attribute of true understanding is the recognition that there is always more to know.

While it is appropriate to state at the beginning that there are exceptions, those exceptions should not be introduced until a basic understanding is acquired and can be applied appropriately to new situations. Teaching a rule and its exceptions at the same time results in confusion and an inadequate degree of original learning, increasing the probability of faulty transfer of that learning to future situations.

TYING EVERYTHING TOGETHER FOR TRANSFER

Teaching for transfer is the hallmark of effectiveness and artistry in our profession. If, after reading this chapter, you feel you need to learn a great deal more about transfer, congratulate yourself on your professional sensitivity. Transfer is a very complex concept and one on which the most sophisticated teachers expend a great deal of time and thought.

In summary, make every attempt to:

- Emphasize similarities that encourage positive transfer.
- Associate students' successful achievement with your content area.
- Use this book to increase your teaching effectiveness, so students achieve a high degree of original learning.

- Identify the critical attributes of the skills, concepts, and generalizations that you teach, so your students can successfully transfer their knowledge to new situations.

If you, the teacher, enthusiastically implement these suggestions, we will have achieved transfer of the basic concepts of mastery teaching to your increasingly excellent professional performance.

Chapter 17

Teaching for Independent Learning

Guide for Group Discussion or Individual Study

Objectives:
Participants will:
a. Discuss the need to teach students to be independent learners in their classes.
b. Identify three independence skills they see the need to teach in class.
c. Identify at least two independent activities of Type 1, 2, or 3 (discussed in the chapter) that could be used in their class.

Anticipatory Set:
a. In your class, do all of the students have the same learning needs? If not, how do they differ?
b. What do you do with the students who already know what you are teaching or are not ready for what you will be teaching?
c. What do students who finish an assignment do while others still need more time to work?

Input & Modeling:
Read the chapter "Teaching for Independent Learning."

Checking for Understanding & Guided Practice:
Revisit the questions in the anticipatory set. Have the participants share the independent skills they see they need to teach in their classes so that they can work with small groups on needed skills.

Have the participants identify different levels of independent activities based on the learning and practice needs of their students.

Independent Practice:
The participants will implement these ideas in their classes.

Chapter 17

Teaching for Independent Learning

Today's schools are filled with a more diverse population than at any other time in our history. Children with different life experiences and from various cultures, economic levels, and family structures arrive in our classrooms. In light of our knowledge of how humans learn, the diversity of what children bring to our classes presents a challenge to our responsibility of providing an appropriate instructional program for each child.

DIFFERENTIATING INSTRUCTION

As we increasingly acknowledge the necessity of assessment driving our instructional practices, the need to differentiate what we teach to meet different student needs becomes apparent. As discussed in earlier chapters, a dependent curriculum sequence demands that students receive instruction at a level where their current learning leaves off in that subject. Unfortunately for our convenience, all students' knowledge for any given age or grade level does not leave off at the same place. As a result, at times we need to tailor instruction to small, flexible groups of students with similar needs. This inevitably raises the following questions:

- While I work with a small group of students, what do I do with the rest of the class?

- How can I concentrate with a small group if I'm constantly interrupted by students who have questions that need answering?
- When I am working with small groups of students, how do I make sure that the rest of the class is productively engaged and not just wasting time?

These questions express valid concerns that arise when we prescribe small-group instruction. Not only do we want the ability to have uninterrupted teaching time to meet the wide needs we face, but we also want the students to have access to quality instruction that moves them predictably forward in achievement.

> *"To meet the needs of all students, we must teach them a set of skills that allows them to function productively, independent of our direct supervision."*

GETTING STUDENTS TO WORK INDEPENDENTLY

To meet the needs of all students, we must teach them a set of skills that allows them to function productively, independent of our direct supervision. *Productively*, as described here, will have a different meaning depending on the grade level of the student. In a primary classroom, a productively engaged student might read quietly with a partner, sort words into rhyming pairs, or create an illustration for a story. In an upper grade classroom, while the teacher works with a small group on increasing description in their writing, other students might have peers edit their first drafts, make revisions, or use a thesaurus to find more interesting descriptive words.

Developing Independent Learners

How do we get our students to be effective independent learners? Just like any other skill we want students to develop, the answer is rooted in quality teaching. We often do a very good job of teaching our students how to read, write, and think mathematically while at the same time we expect them to behave in a way that allows the classroom to function smoothly. If we apply the same principles that we know are effective in teaching academic curriculum to the teaching of behavior, we can achieve remarkable results.

Independence as a Subject

Think of independence as another of our content areas that needs teaching. Like any other complex learning, it is made up of subskills, which are necessary for the student to become productively independent. Independence is a content area that is best taught at the beginning of the school year (although it can be taught at any time) so that the benefits of independent learners carry throughout the year. In many effective classrooms, the skills of independence are the priority of all instructional efforts (over academics) for the first two to four weeks of class. It is this high allocation of time to the teaching of the skills of independence that allows teachers to devote even more time to academic instruction throughout the rest of the school year.

Classroom Procedures and Skills

For the students to function independently, they need to be taught both classroom procedures and the skills that allow them to proactively self-direct their attention and effort when not under the teacher's direct supervision. Classroom procedures consist of the routines, organization, and practices that characterize daily classroom life:

- How do we enter the classroom?
- What do we do when we first enter?
- Where are the materials needed for daily work?
- What do we do with completed work?
- What do we do with work in progress?
- What do we do when we finish an assignment?
- What is needed on the heading of a paper?

All of these, and more, are procedures that need to be taught each year. One would expect that by the time the students reach the middle grades these would be in place. However, each teacher does things differently (even if slightly), and each teacher has different expectations that need to be taught to a new group of students. These procedures are the *how* of what is to be happening in the classroom.

The Perfect Class

What would you see if you were a visitor in a classroom where the teacher has taught the students to work productively and independently while the teacher is working with other students? The teacher could be working with a small group of students or having individual conferences with students. The rest of the students would be engaged individually, in pairs, or in cooperative groups, on tasks that are relevant and worthwhile for their learning needs. Conversations would be at a very low level and only as necessary for the task at hand. Students would go to the supply area and get or return materials as they changed from one activity (or part of the task) to another. They would maintain a high level of concentration on the task.

There might be a number of student needs, such as sharpening pencils, getting a drink, using the restroom, getting a tissue, or going to a counselor or resource teacher at a specified time. All of this would be done without the direct supervision of the teacher and in such a way that everyone could continue working without interruption.

You would not see students staring into space, sitting with a hand in the air waiting for the teacher, interrupting the teacher (except in the case of an emergency), making toys out of classroom supplies, or engaging in activities that were not educationally productive at the time (e.g., doodling, having social conversations, reading comic books and popular magazines). You would not hear the teacher saying, "It is getting too noisy in the back of the room" or "We have already talked about what to do when you finish your assignment" or "You just came in from lunch; you should have used the restroom then."

In a successful classroom, students are taught to be autonomous, self-reliant, independent learners. As a result, the teacher has uninterrupted time to attend to the educational needs of a small group of learners or individual students.

Creating the Perfect Class

How do we go about creating such a productive learning environment? After developing the vision of your ideal classroom, you must identify the specific skills that students would need to operate independently in that classroom. Different grade levels, subject areas, and teaching and learning styles may influence the skills students need. The following are examples of some of those skills:

The Learner

- has demonstrated the skills to do the task without assistance.
- responds to the class signal when the teacher needs to get everyone's attention for clarification or additional information.
- gets necessary materials.
- follows directions/rules/procedures for the task.
- gets started quickly.
- goes to the appropriate source for help (self, peers, materials, teacher).
- works so that others can continue working.
- works without unnecessary distraction.

- moves around the room so that others can continue working.
- returns to the task quickly after distraction.
- selects an appropriate place to work (if given the option).
- chooses appropriate new work when a task is completed and there is still time to work.
- uses materials appropriately.
- returns materials appropriately.
- completes the task according to appropriate criteria.
- takes care of personal needs according to class procedures.
- gets directions for activities from written or pictorial instructions.

These are the foundation skills that need to be taught so that students can work independently on academic tasks of increasing demand. Remember that these skills must be adapted to your specific students and classroom organization. There is tremendous variety in what you will see in classrooms where the teachers have taken the time to teach students to be independent learners.

> *"Think of independence as another of our content areas that needs teaching. Like any other complex learning, it is made up of smaller subskills...."*

Three Activity Types for Independent Learning

When we look at the kinds of tasks students do independently at school, they fall into three basic activity groups.

Type 1 Activities

These are the activities that encourage students to be productively engaged without direct teacher supervision. The primary learning is that of taking care of oneself for a period of time. These are usually fun, higher interest activities that students know how to do already: playing games, working puzzles, coloring, looking at a book, listening at the listening center, drawing, playing with pattern blocks, and so on. There is little or no academic learning occurring. These activities are only used as a vehicle for teaching students the skills needed to be an independent, self-directed learner. All of the teacher's feedback to the students (knowledge of results) is focused on how well the students are doing with the skills of working independently.

Type 2 Activities

These are activities that require students to be productively engaged in academic tasks without direct teacher supervision. Students practice previously learned academic skills with which they need to increase accuracy, speed, or facility. These activities might include reading, independent practice from a lesson that just concluded, phonics games, flashcards, vocabulary concentration, handwriting practice, math problem-solving activities, writing and grammar exercises, and so on.

In these activities, there is a balance between practicing taking care of oneself and practicing previously learned academic skills. The teacher's feedback to the students would be balanced between the quality of the academic work and the skills of working independently.

Type 3 Activities

These activities require students to extend previous learning or pursue new learning on their own. The activities can be self-selected or assigned. Activities of this type could include reading in a new subject area and preparing a written or oral report, following directions for and carrying out a science investigation, designing a game that other students could use to practice their math fact families, writing a student play to be performed, and so on.

This type of activity requires a great deal of independence. However, just as we continually increase the level of difficulty for academic learning, we need to continually encourage higher levels of independence. We can achieve this by periodically providing students with feedback on how well they are doing as independent learners as well as the quality of their academic work.

As the activities move from Type 1 to Type 3, there is an increasing shift in focus from high demand for self-reliance to high demand for academic growth. If the students cannot maintain themselves with Type 1 activities, increasing academic demand will only confound the situation. Usually, in the primary grades, we start this process with Type 1 activities, and, as the students learn to self-direct their focus and effort, we escalate the demand to more academic (Type 2) activities. In the upper grades, even though the students are more academically capable, if they cannot maintain self-direction, Type 1 activities are the place to start in teaching independence skills.

Social Complexities

With each of these types of activities, we increase the demand on the student if we add other students into the mix. Having a student work alone on a task is far easier than working with another student or group of students. Now, in addition to the skills of self-reliance, we are adding the dimension of social skills. As stated earlier, beginning this process at the start of the school year pays great dividends.

PLANNING FOR YOUR STUDENTS' INDEPENDENT LEARNING

Now that you have a vision of what independent learners look like in a classroom and the skills of independence they need, identify which procedures you'll want to initially establish. Plan a lesson in which you teach one procedure to the class. That procedure becomes the objective of the lesson. Teach the procedure, model it, and check the students' understanding of the procedure.

Practice the Procedure

If we abandon any other efforts in procedure instruction, we can predict that we'll be constantly reminding our students of the procedure. Instead of leaving instruction after checking for understanding, design a period in which the students practice the procedure. Be it entering the room, reading and following directions from the chalkboard, responding to a class signal, or having appropriate materials out, the students need practice in which all of their neural energy is focused on that procedure or skill. Any materials you have them use and assignments or activities you have them do are just vehicles for practicing that particular procedure.

The teacher should be circulating or be in an appropriate position to watch and provide specific knowledge of results on the students' efforts with that procedure. Remember the generalization applying to effective practice: For fast learning, we mass practice (i.e., schedule short, frequent practices close together, with feedback). For the first couple of days, most of your focus and feedback will be on the procedures you have taught and continue to practice. Soon the students will have internalized them to the point that they are occurring regularly. Only an infrequent mention is now required to keep the procedure sharp; then new procedures can be taught.

DISENGAGING WHILE WORKING IN SMALL GROUPS

Now that the students are beginning to follow classroom routines and procedures independently and you have some academic assessment data, you may see the need to work with smaller groups of students. When first beginning to pull a small group for instruction, your objective is not to instruct the small group but to withdraw yourself from direct supervision of the rest of the class. The unsupervised students need to get used to not having you controlling all of the activity.

When with the small group, your attention will initially be on what the rest of the class is doing while they're not with you. Using your radar to watch how well students remain focused, periodically leave the small group (with a task to do while you are gone) and circulate. Provide positive reinforcement to the students who are remaining on task; then keep moving. Gradually you will see the students' increased ability to productively self-direct their efforts while you are not in charge.

A teacher working with small groups becomes off limits (unless there is a loss of blood or lack of breathing!) to the rest of the class, so the small groups can be taught uninterrupted. This is why it is important to spend time practicing with students and teaching them what to do when they encounter problems of various kinds. What do they do when they don't have the pencil they need, when they become stuck on a problem or assignment, when they disagree with their partner, or when they need to leave the classroom? When alternative solutions are taught and the students are held accountable for using them, they quickly learn to remove roadblocks and move on.

ENSURING INDEPENDENT LEARNING

As you can see, independence is far more complex than just telling students, "Go work on this quietly at your seat." Independence requires teaching a complex set of skills, but we do this for reading, writing, and mathematics. The difference is that too many educators view academic skills as something the students do not already know, and it is our job as teachers to teach them. Educators view the skills of being independent as skills the students should be able to do and not something that needs teaching.

Too often students are admonished to be more responsible and independent but not taught how. All too often we find that students do not have these skills, do not gain them by being told to use them, and will learn them very quickly when we systematically teach them. When we have a class of independent learners, our students can be productively engaged in a wide variety of self-directed activities accomplished individually, with a partner, or in cooperative learning groups. At the same time, other students can receive instruction tailored to meet their needs in a small group or individually.

It is very gratifying to see the considerable increase in our students' skills of independence and time on productive learning activities, as well as more productive small-group instruction. An additional, very powerful reason for investing time in teaching for independent learning is the calmer, more relaxed, and less stressful atmosphere for both the students and the teacher.

Recommended Reading

Ainsworth, L. (2003) *Power standards: Identifying the standards that matter the most.* Denver, CO: Advanced Learning Centers.

Bandura, A. (1997). *Self-efficacy: The exercise of control.* New York: W.H. Freeman.

Bloom, B. (Ed.). (1956). *Taxonomy of educational objectives: The classification of educational goals. Handbook I: Cognitive domain.* New York: David McKay.

Brandt, R. (1998). *Powerful learning.* Alexandria, VA: Association for Supervision and Curriculum Development.

Bruer, J. (1994). *Schools for thought: A science of learning in the classroom.* Cambridge, MA: MIT Press.

Bruner, J. (1996). *The culture of education.* Cambridge, MA: Harvard University Press.

Caine, R. N., & Caine, G. (1994). *Making connections: Teaching and the human brain.* Reading, MA: Addison-Wesley.

Caine, R. N., & Caine, G. (1997). *Education on the edge of possibility.* Alexandria, VA: Association for Supervision and Curriculum Development.

Costa, A. (1991). *The school as a home for the mind.* Arlington Heights, IL: Skylight Publishing.

Costa, A., & Garmston, R. (1994). *The art of cognitive coaching.* Norwood, MA: Christopher Gordon.

Costa, A., & Garmston, R. (2002). *Cognitive coaching: A foundation for renaissance schools.* Norwood, MA: Christopher Gordon.

Csikszentmihalyi, M. (1990). *Flow: The psychology of optimal experience.* New York: Harper & Row.

Csikszentmihalyi, M. (1997). *Creativity: Flow and the psychology of discovery and invention.* New York: HarperCollins.

Dewey, J. (1916). *Democracy and education: An introduction to the philosophy of education.* New York: Macmillan.

Dewey, J. (1933). *How we think: A restatement of the relation of reflective thinking to the educative process.* Boston: Henry Holt.

Dewey, J. (1937). *Experience in education.* New York: Macmillan.

Eisner, E. W. (1994). *Cognition and curriculum reconsidered.* New York: Teachers College Press.

Erickson, L. (2001). *Stirring the head, heart, and soul: Redefining curriculum and instruction* (2nd ed.). Thousand Oaks, CA: Corwin.

Erickson, L. (2002). *Concept-based curriculum and instruction: Teaching beyond the facts.* Thousand Oaks, CA: Corwin.

Fogarty, R., & Bellanca, J. (1993). *Patterns for thinking, patterns for transfer: A cooperative team approach for critical and creative thinking in the classroom.* Arlington Heights, Illinois: IRI/Skylight Publishing.

Gambrell, L. B., Morrow, L. M., Neuman, S. B., & Pressley, M. (1999). *Best practices in literacy instruction.* New York: Guilford.

Gardner, H. (1983). *Frames of mind: The theory of multiple intelligences.* New York: Basic Books.

Gardner, H. (1991). *The unschooled mind: How children think and how schools should teach.* New York: Basic Books.

Gardner, H. (1993). *Multiple intelligences: The theory in practice.* New York: Basic Books.

Given, B. K. (2002). *The brain's natural learning systems.* Alexandria, VA: Association for Supervision and Curriculum Development.

Glasser, W. (1990). *The quality school: Managing students without coercion.* New York: Perennial Library.

Glasser, W. (1998). *Choice theory in the classroom.* New York: HarperPerennial.

Gregorc, A. F. (1985). *Inside styles: beyond the basics: Questions and answers on style.* Maynard, MA: Gabriel Systems.

Gregory, G. H., & Chapman, C. (2002). *Differentiated instructional strategies: One size doesn't fit all.* Thousand Oaks, CA: Corwin.

Hunter, M. (1967). *Teach more–Faster!* Thousand Oaks, CA: Corwin.

Hunter, M. (1969). *Improved instruction.* Thousand Oaks, CA: Corwin.

Hunter, M. (1969). *Motivation theory for teachers.* Thousand Oaks, CA: Corwin.

Hunter, M. (1982). *Mastery teaching: Increasing instructional effectiveness in elementary and secondary schools, colleges, and universities.* Thousand Oaks, CA: Corwin.

Hunter, M. (1990). *Discipline that develops self-discipline.* Thousand Oaks, CA: Corwin.

Hunter, M. (1994). *Enhancing teaching.* New York: Macmillan.

Hunter, M. (1995). *Teach for transfer.* Thousand Oaks, CA: Corwin.

Hunter, M., & Breit, S. (1969). *Aide-ing in education.* Thousand Oaks, CA: Corwin.

Hunter, M., & Carlson, P. V. (1994). *Improving your child's behavior.* Thousand Oaks, CA: Corwin.

Hunter, M., & Russell, D. (1989). *Mastering coaching and supervision.* Thousand Oaks, CA: Corwin.

Jacobs, H. H. (1997). *Mapping the big picture: Integrating curriculum and assessment K–12.* Alexandria, VA: Association for Supervision and Curriculum Development.

Jensen, E. (1995). *Brain-based learning and teaching.* Del Mar, CA: Turning Point.

Jensen, E. (1998). *Teaching with the brain in mind.* Alexandria, VA: Association for Supervision and Curriculum Development.

Johnson, D., & Johnson, R. (1991). *Cooperative learning lesson structures.* Edina, MN: Interaction Books.

Johnson, D., & Johnson, R. (1998). *Learning together and alone* (5th ed.). Boston: Allyn & Bacon.

Kauchak, D. P., & Eggen, P. (1998). *Learning and teaching: Research-based methods* (3rd ed.). Boston: Allyn & Bacon.

Kessler, R. (2000). *The soul of education: Helping students find connection, compassion, and character at school.* Alexandria, VA: Association for Supervision and Curriculum Development.

Lawrence, G., & Hunter, M. (1978). *Parent-teacher conferencing.* Thousand Oaks, CA: Corwin.

Marzano, R. (2003). *What works in schools: Translating research into action.* Alexandria, Virginia: Association for Supervision and Curriculum Development.

Marzano, R., Pickering, D. J., & Pollack, J. E. (2000). *Classroom instruction that works: Research-based strategies for increasing student achievement.* Alexandria, VA: Association for Supervision and Curriculum Development.

Noddings, N. (1992). *The challenge to care in schools.* New York: Teachers College Press.

Perkins, D. (1992). *Smart schools: From training memories to educating minds.* New York: Free Press.

Perkins, D. (1994). *Knowledge as design: A book for critical and creative discussion across the curriculum.* Pacific Grove, CA: Critical Thinking Press.

Perkins, D. (1995). *Outsmarting IQ: The emerging science of learnable intelligence.* New York: Free Press.

Piaget, J. (1952). *The origins of intelligence in children.* New York: International Universities Press.

Pressley, M. (1998). *Reading instruction that works: The case for balanced teaching* (2nd ed.). New York: Guilford.

Reeves, D. B. (2000). *Accountability in action: A blueprint for learning organizations.* Denver, CO: Advanced Learning Press.

Scheidecker, D., & Freeman, W. (1999). *Bringing out the best in students: How legendary teachers motivate kids.* Thousand Oaks, CA: Corwin.

Shulman, J. H. (Ed.). (1992). *Case methods in teacher education.* New York: Teachers College Press.

Siegler, R. S. (1998). *Children's thinking* (3rd ed.). Upper Saddle River, NJ: Prentice Hall.

Silver, H., Strong, R., & Perini, M. (2000). *So each may learn: Integrating learning Styles and multiple intelligences.* Alexandria, VA: Association for Supervision and Curriculum Development.

Smith, F. (1990). *To think.* New York: Teachers College Press.

Sousa, D. (2001). *How the brain learns.* Thousand Oaks, CA: Corwin.

Sprenger, M. (1999). *Learning and memory: The brain in action.* Alexandria, VA: Association for Supervision and Curriculum Development.

Sternberg, R. (1985). *Beyond IQ: A triarchic theory of human intelligence.* New York: Cambridge University Press.

Sternberg, R. (1996). *Successful intelligence: How practical and creative intelligence determine success in life.* New York: Simon & Schuster.

Stiggins, R. J. (1997). Student-centered classroom assessment (2nd ed.). Columbus, OH: Merrill.

Stigler, J. W., & Hiebert, J. (1999). *The teaching gap: Best ideas from the world's teachers for improving education in the classroom.* New York: Free Press.

Sylwester, R. A. (1995). *Celebration of neurons: An educator's guide to the human brain.* Alexandria, VA: Association for Supervision and Curriculum Development.

Sylwester, R. (2003). *A biological brain in a cultural classroom* (2nd ed.). Thousand Oaks, CA: Corwin.

Thornburg, D. (2002). *The new basics education and the future of work in the telematic age.* Alexandria, VA: Association for Supervision and Curriculum Development.

Tomlinson, C. A. (1999). *The differentiated classroom: Responding to the needs of all learners.* Alexandria, VA: Association for Supervision and Curriculum Development.

Tomlinson, C. A. (2002). *How to differentiate instruction in mixed-ability classrooms* (2nd ed.). Alexandria, VA: Association for Supervision and Curriculum Development.

Tomlinson, C. A., Kaplan, S. N., Renzulli, J. S., Purcell, J., Leppien, J., & Burns, D. (2002). *The parallel curriculum: A design to develop high potential and challenge high-ability learners.* Thousand Oaks, CA: Corwin.

Vygotsky, L. S. (1986). *Thought and language* (rev. ed.). Cambridge, MA: Harvard University Press.

Vygotsky, L. S., Vygotsky, S., & John-Steiner, V. (Eds.). (1978). *Mind in society: The development of higher psychological processes.* Cambridge, MA: Harvard University Press.

Wasley, P., Hampel, R., & Clark, R. (1997). *Kids and school reform.* San Francisco: Jossey-Bass.

Wiggins, G. (1998). *Educative assessment: Designing assessments to inform and improve performance.* Alexandria, VA: Association for Supervision and Curriculum Development.

Wiggins, G., & McTighe, J. (1998). *Understanding by design.* Alexandria, VA: Association for Supervision and Curriculum Development.

Wolfe, P. (2001). *Brain matters: Translating research into classroom practice.* Alexandria, VA: Association for Supervision and Curriculum Development.

Index